What's Next?

Media Studies Series

1968: Year of Media Decision
edited by Robert Giles and Robert W. Snyder

America's Schools and the Mass Media,
edited by Everette E. Dennis and Craig L. LaMay

Children and the Media,
edited by Everette E. Dennis and Edward C. Pease

Covering China,
edited by Robert W. Snyder

Covering Congress,
edited by Everette E. Dennis and Robert W. Snyder

The Culture of Crime,
edited by Everette E. Dennis and Craig L. LaMay

Defining Moments in Journalism,
edited by Nancy J. Woodhull and Robert W. Snyder

Higher Education in the Information Age,
edited by Everette E. Dennis and Craig L. LaMay

Journalists in Peril,
edited by Nancy J. Woodhull and Robert W. Snyder

The Media in Black and White,
edited by Everette E. Dennis and Edward C. Pease

Media and Democracy,
edited by Everette E. Dennis and Robert W. Snyder

Media Mergers,
edited by Nancy J. Wood hull and Robert W. Snyder

Media and Public Life,
edited by Everette E. Dennis and Edward C. Pease

Profiles in Journalistic Courage
edited by Robert Giles, Robert W. Snyder and Lisa DeLisle

Publishing Books,
edited by Everette E. Dennis, Craig L. LaMay, and Edward C. Pease

Radio—The Forgotten Medium,
edited by Edward C. Pease and Everette E. Dennis

Reporting the Post-Communist Revolution
edited by Robert Giles & Robert W. Snyder

What's Fair? The Problem of Equity in Journalism
edited by Robert Giles and Robert W. Snyder

What's Next? The Problem and Prospects of Journalism
edited by Robert Giles and Robert W. Snyder

Problems & Prospects of Journalism

What's Next?

Robert Giles
Robert W. Snyder
editors

Transaction Publishers
New Brunswick (U.S.A.) and London (U.K.)

This book is printed on acid-free paper that meets the American National
Standard for Permanence of Paper for Printed Library Materials.

Library of Congress Catalog Number: 00-061529
ISBN:0–7658–0709–2
Printed in the United States of America

Library of Congress Cataloging-in-Publication Data

What's next? : the problems and prospects of journalism / Robert Giles and
Robert W. Snyder, editors.
    p.   cm. — (Media studies series)
Originally published : The media studies journal, Spring/Summer 1999.
Includes index.
ISBN 0-7658-0709-2 (pbk. : alk. paper)
    1. Journalism. 2. Electronic newspapers. 3. Electronic news gathering.
I. Giles, Robert H., 1933–   II. Snyder, Robert W., 1955–   III. Series

PN4731.W49 2000
070.4—dc21   00-061529

Contents

Preface   *xi*

Futures

Letter from the Future—I   3
   Elizabeth Weise
Imagining the journalism of 2025, a writer foresees a world where the media condition the public "to pay attention only to their narrow interests, presented as entertainment."

Letter from the Future—II   9
   Geneva Overholser
Looking ahead to 2025, a columnist foresees renewal for newspapers when they begin to see themselves as "a nucleus in the multidimensional atom of communication."

The Future Is the Net   15
   Jon Katz
"The Web is the central reality—economic, social, cultural, political— for younger generations," argues a media critic, "whether we like it or not, whether we think it is a good thing or not. I don't think the Web is supplanting culture; it is creating new culture."

Lawyers, Voyeurs and Vigilantes   19
   James W. Carey
In the aftermath of the Clinton scandal, a scholar offers a warning: "When journalists measure their success solely by the size of their readership or audience, by the profits of their companies or by their

incomes, status and visibility, they have caved in to the temptation of worshipping false gods, of selling their heritage for a pottage—just as much as those who cynically convinced themselves they were serving democracy by acting as the mouthpieces of a putatively revolutionary party."

Who?

Who Will Be Journalists in the Next Century?   29
    David Weaver

An authority on the demography of American journalists looks at major trends and concludes: "The journalists of the next century will be more representative of the larger U.S. society demographically than those of this past century. They will also be more formally educated and more inclined to be independent thinkers who cannot be easily duped or manipulated."

Who's a Journalist?—I   39
    Ted Gup

"Who is a journalist? Some will say that the question is elitist, that it comes from a profession intent upon protecting its franchise, like some medieval guild that awakens to discover history has passed it by," writes a journalism professor. "But there is nothing elitist or anti-democratic about believing that the public is entitled to the very best information, that it benefits from trained observers who understand not only the demands of meeting deadlines, but also the virtues of restraint, of confirmation, of accuracy, balance and fairness."

Who's a Journalist?—II   45
    Mike Godwin

"I'm trying not to be too much of a sappy utopian here," writes an author committed to civil liberties in cyberspace, "but if I squint hard enough, I can see a future transformed by an Everyman Journalism that combines the best of traditional news organizations with all the diverse knowledge and insight of a global newsroom on the World Wide Web."

What?

Magazines   53
  David Abrahamson

"In the '90s, a decade defined by the globalization of commerce and communication, magazines are now in the middle of a new evolution, one distinguished by niche marketing and fertile interaction between print media and the World Wide Web," writes an authority on magazines. "Where these latest developments will take us is not entirely clear, but it is certain that magazines will both capitalize on and transcend their own recent history."

Network and Cable TV   63
  Kyle Pope

"Beyond the decline of broadcast network news as we have known it, a much more revolutionary change is unfolding," writes a media reporter. "For today's big broadcast and cable networks, the arrival of digital TV represents a brutal leveling of the playing field."

Newspapers   71
  Leo Bogart

"Even if the Internet had not arrived on the scene," a media analyst argues, "newspapers would still be undergoing profound changes over the next quarter-century—some forced by the environment and some imposed by their own efforts to remain responsive to readers and advertisers. The trends that will affect the metropolitan daily press are already well established."

When?

What's the Rush?   83
  Dave Kansas and Todd Gitlin

Is concern over the 24–hour news cycle "nervous carping" or sensible skepticism? The editor of an on-line financial news organization and a professor of culture, journalism and sociology debate each other.

Where?

Business News and International Reporting   91
   Richard Lambert

International news is not disappearing, it is changing its configuration, argues the editor of a business newspaper: "Just as the old model of international news reporting, based on bureaus of general correspondents, has moved into a stage of rapid decline, so the business news organizations have been expanding their networks of specialist correspondents around the world at a hectic pace."

New Wars, New Correspondents   97
   Stacy Sullivan

"Sadly," writes a correspondent who has reported from the Balkans, "I have seen the future of foreign reporting—it is Kosovo. I can only hope that the system by which the American news media covers the world will be reformed."

A Web of Sound   103
   Kenneth R. Donow and Peggy Miles

"The encounter between radio and the Internet raises transforming possibilities," two radio analysts write. "From the vantage point of people who seek a wide range of news sources on the radio, news reports issuing over the Internet from local markets around the world will become a new and valued first source of information on many stories of critical concern."

Why?

New News, New Ideas   111
   Compiled by Jennifer Kelley

Six deans—David Rubin, Orville Schell, Ken Bode, Geoffrey Cowan, Terry Hynes, Robert Ruggles and Tom Goldstein—offer insights on educating the journalists of the future. "We still have to make them excited," Rubin says, "about being the public's eyes and ears, about being an essential part of the American democratic process, about representing the voiceless and the underdog, about being an adversary or at least a watchdog of power and about recognizing that they are in this business not for the money but for the contribution they make to the overall health of the country."

Gnats Chasing an Elephant   121
    James Boylan

"The terms of press criticism remain unsettled," writes a former journalism review editor. "Yet as we approach a new century we have become less certain that we are doing good, less certain of our agenda, less certain of appropriate forms. The time may be at hand for unblinking re-evaluation."

The Bumpy Road of Regulation   129
    Stuart N. Brotman

"Although much of the focus of this process of reinventing the FCC is on telecommunications rather than electronic media," writes an authority on communications law, "the broad and deep impact of this 'less regulation, less government' paradigm shift also is destined to change the role of the FCC as it oversees program content regulation for broadcast radio and television news and public affairs programming."

Review Essay

Peering Forward   139
    Christopher Dornan

"If the sheer prominence of the media in all their multiplying aspects is a badge of the present, we shouldn't be surprised if the media prove to be architectural agents of the onrushing future," writes a media studies scholar. "But what will a world shaped by media imperatives look like, what place will journalism occupy in such a future, and did anyone see it coming?"

For Further Reading   151

Index   155

Preface

What's Next?

THE FUTURE OF journalism isn't what it used to be. As recently as the mid-1960s, few would have predicted the shocks and transformations that have swept through the news business in the last three decades: the deaths of many afternoon newspapers, the emergence of television as people's primary news source and the quicksilver combinations of cable television, VCRs and the Internet that have changed our ways of reading, seeing and listening. And then there is the very nature of news reports—so different from what they once were in living memory that Marvin Kalb, viewing uneven sourcing, hasty judgments and celebrity journalists, concludes that we are seeing the rise of a "new news."

If there is one lesson from the surprises of recent decades, it is that we cannot take the future for granted. Another lesson, though, is that it is very difficult to determine what is around the next bend in the road—especially in a field as integrally connected with changes in culture, politics, technology and economics as journalism.

With these cautions in mind, the essays in this volume seek to illuminate the future prospects of journalism, particularly American journalism. Mindful that grandiose predictions of the world of tomorrow tend to be the fantasies and phobias of the present written large— in the '30s and '40s magazines such as Scribner's, Barron's and Collier's forecast that one day we would have an airplane in every garage—we have taken a more careful view.

Our writers start with what we know—the trends that we see in journalism today—and ask where they will take us in the foreseeable future. For some media, such as newspapers, the visible horizon is decades away. For others, particularly anything involving the Internet, responsible forecasts can look ahead only for a matter of years. (There is no getting around the fact that if there is one trend that defines the future of all media, it is their interaction with the computer and the Internet.) Where the likely destinations of present trends are not entirely clear, we have tried to pose the kinds of questions that we believe people will have to address in years to come.

"THE FUTURE," JAMES W. CAREY has written, "whether it appears in the rhetoric of the Left or Right, whether as postmodernism or postindustrialism, is one more device for evading the active role our imaginings of the past and future play in the control of the present." We agree. And because we believe the future that we imagine plays a large role in the actions we take today, we have opened this collection of essays with "Futures," a series of meditations on the tomorrows of journalism. Letters written by Elizabeth Weise and Geneva Overholser imagine the worst and best possibilities for journalism in the year 2025. Jon Katz argues that the future of journalism is on the Internet. James W. Carey offers a warning about the course of journalism and democracy as America moves into a post impeachment landscape.

The remainder of the collection, in an effort to bring new answers to old questions, is organized around the five traditional reporter's questions—who, what, when, where and why.

In "Who?" David Weaver looks at the demographic trends in American journalism to venture some predictions on who the journalists of the next century will be. Ted Gup and Mike Godwin, writing in the shadow cast over the future of journalism by Matt Drudge, present contrasting perspectives on the question of who is a journalist.

In "What?" David Abrahamson looks at the prospects of magazines, Kyle Pope examines the future of network and cable television, and Leo Bogart offers newspapers advice on how to survive in the next millennium.

In "When?" Todd Gitlin and Dave Kansas conduct an epistolary debate, by e-mail, on the 24-hour news cycle.

In "Where?" Richard Lambert analyzes the role of business news in defining the emerging face of international reporting. Stacy Sullivan ponders the lessons of her own experiences covering conflict in the Balkans as one of many stringers working without the benefit of a full-time affiliation with a major news organization. Kenneth R. Donow and Peggy Miles explore the intersection of radio and the Internet and its consequences for international news.

In "Why?" we present thoughts on the education of future journalists from six deans: David Rubin, Orville Schell, Ken Bode, Geoffrey

Cowan, Terry Hynes, Robert Ruggles and Tom Goldstein. James Boylan looks at the evolution of the underlying premises of press criticism, while Stuart N. Brotman examines the likely future of FCC regulation of broadcast radio, television news and public affairs programming.

Christopher Dornan concludes this volume with a review essay on major books of the last century depicting the future in general and the media and journalism in particular.

If these many imaginings have one lesson, it is this: the future of journalism will not be ordained by technology, punditry or market share. Rather, it will be determined by the sum of countless actions taken here and now by journalists and people who care about journalism. These essays, with their hopes and fears, cautions and enthusiasms, questions and answers, directives and exhortations, are our effort to create the best possible future for journalism.

—The Editors

Futures

*Journalism really needs to survive, especially in
this age where there is so much information from so many
different places.*—JON KATZ

Letter from the Future—I

Journalism in 2025 isn't pretty.

Elizabeth Weise

May 1, 2025

DEAR JOSE,

So you want the lowdown on life in the trenches, eh? It's not pretty—not that it ever was—but it's much worse than when we worked together in the '90s, back before you went off to teach masscomm. But if you've got students who want to be filers, what they used to call reporters, I can give you the dirt.

First off, they can forget working in clean news like the *Times*, unless their parents work there or they went to Harvard. And even then, they need serious family money. At plenty of prestige papers and magazines, the only way in is to join a pool of supplicants who work for almost nothing for almost three years in the vain hope that you'll be the one person who gets a permanent job at the end of the stint. If you're a winner, great. But everyone else gets nothing but clips and debt. And they don't hire from the feeds*.

There really aren't anything but contract jobs anymore unless you're in management, and then it's just a contract with stock options. And tell them they want short-term contracts in the beginning, so they can fight for more money when they're up for renewal. I've seen newbies get stuck in five-year contracts at ridiculous wages.

At someplace like Yahoo the contracts are for filers or readers. Filers actually cover news and file into a template. An algorithm decides how each story gets sliced and diced for the independent news feeds. Then the readers read the finished product to make sure it scans.

3

You haven't lived until you've seen 23 different versions of a shootout, each for a different indie** feed: tabloid, sexy, pious, enviro, bloodngore, G-rated, all-pictures, all-sound, English, Spanish and Official. It numbs the mind.

Which is good, because that way you don't pay attention to the facts of the story, which change more than slightly depending on whose ads are paying for it. I've seen stuff go through the agroindustry trade association filter that would make your DNA uncurl (and probably has).

You know that little "incident" down at the Monslamo biopharmaceutical plant in Gilroy? I was there. I saw what happened to the kids. I filed stories for three straight days and not one made it into the feed. Not one. The pictures did. They were too good to hold back. Genes that were never meant to jump from one species to another somehow did—straight into the guts of those toddlers. They had these huge goiters; the poor kids walked like the things were going to tip them over. I wanted to tell the whole story, but if I took it to someplace other than the feed I usually work for they would have sued me for breach of contract.

Which brings us to free-lance contracts, which mean more freedom but also more uncertainty. The maw of the news beast is so large it seems like there'd be work for everyone. But it's only certain kinds of work, certain kinds of stories. Most of the free-lancers I know have a specific beat they cover and have made peace with their consciences, or they're just astoundingly poor. Or they join a news collective, like I did. The collective brokers deals between free-lancers and media outlets; otherwise you spend so much time making deals that you can't do any work.

The collectives are about creating a single unified product they can sell to the feeds, no matter how many different filers they've got working for them, so that means getting used to working with a simulacrum. You do one story with those nasty little transponder dots pasted on your face, then the program records all your facial movements, morphs it onto five or 10 different sims, and it gets sold to 20 different feeds.

Our main simulacrum's nice, Larry Keller. You must have seen him, even up there. He fronted all the Macrosurf bankruptcy stuff two years ago. Blond, Midwest corn-fed kind of creature. Nice low voice that carries well on the handhelds, which is good for breaking stuff.

It took me awhile to get used to working with a sim. I used to like doing my own reports, my face out there for all the world to see. Except of course all the world didn't want to see my smiling-and-aging Chinese face. They wanted a white guy. Or a buxom redhead. Or a Mexican with a Toltec nose like yours. Something familiar.

The people watching the news do realize that the sims aren't real, don't they? I wonder sometimes. Have you seen those surveys that show how people wildly overestimate their numbers in the population as a whole? It's because everything they see—the ads, the news, the shows—are all sims morphed to mirror them. Something like 75 percent of white folks still think they're in the majority. Can you believe it?

Doing sims did wonders for my standard of living. Once you get into it, money starts plinking into your account like a cloud burst. Great. I finally own my own condo. But I'm still bitter.

Do your students know what they're getting into? They think it's like in the movies, all Peace Barrymore and Ashley DiCaprio. It's terrifying how little they understand about how the world works.

I talked to the daughter of a friend, who actually thought there was a human editor somewhere deciding what news she saw, instead of an algorithm that analyzed the stories she'd looked at in the past, the products she'd bought, the videos she'd downloaded, the songs she'd listened to, the ads she'd checked out and the answers she gave to those little "fun" surveys that pop up on her on her screen now and again. They know what we want better than we know ourselves. She was kind of deliciously grossed out when I told her what she saw was only about making her spend more time glued to her screen.

You can pay for clean news, but it's expensive. What's a subscription to the *Times* these days, a month's rent? Some of the enviros who follow politics claim their stuff's less corporate, but it's still as spun as anything else, just a different way.

Information's always available—it's not like they're keeping anything from people. It's just that the public doesn't care because they're conditioned to pay attention only to their narrow interests, presented as entertainment.

Investigative work still gets done, but good luck finding someplace to run your stuff. All these feeds are owned by big huge industrial gorillas that do everything from manufacture cars to make movies. They don't even pretend that old church/state line exists anymore.

Which means to sell your story, you've got to figure out which feed is owned by a company who wants to give another company bad press.

You can't even find good sources anymore. Remember the Great Genes/BioBaby merger, when it was suddenly going to get so cheap to make sure your embryo didn't have any bad DNA? One of the docs I talked to said he's pretty sure the process also built bad DNA into the embryo, with ramifications we won't see for one or two generations. But he can't be sure because all the university funding sources are corporate now, and what corporation is going to pay to find out that its new revenue stream is going to create a bunch of Down's kids in 70 years? No source, no story. No story, no uproar. No uproar and your grandkid's got an IQ of 50. But by then BioBaby will have done an overseas bankruptcy and popped back up under some new name, as unsueable as one of those perfect newborns they use in their ads.

But as bad as all that is, I think the local angle is worse. There just isn't a market for local investigative stuff any more. Those are the stories no one but public officials ever read anyway, so you can't sell them to save your life. The cops are roughing up Vietnamese kids at a local club in Carson City. Who cares? Even if you dig up something, who's going to bother when local stories pay next to nothing, and the local feeds are pretty much blinking wrapping for ads?

Everything is about "economies of scale," and any town under 250,000 just doesn't measure up as worth the bandwidth. It's all so fragmented that you can't figure your specific feed's getting more than a couple of hundred from any one town, so unless the story's of interest to a bigger area it just isn't going to make it.

So much stuff gets hidden in plain sight now. Big blowups, big massacres—we cover those because the pictures are good and people like a little bloodngore with their dinner. But if you really want to kill a whole bunch of people, you just do it slowly and nobody notices a thing. It took China six years to relocate the Mongolians, yurt by yurt, and no one did a thing about it because they didn't know it was happening. I suppose the clean news feeds said something, but they've got, what, 3 percent of the viewers? And their viewers are probably the people making money off the new Mongolian wheat crops anyway.

There's just no possibility of a national consensus on much of anything these days, because the nation doesn't have any one single reference point. They get so much junk thrown at them they have the illusion they're well informed. We've done such a good job of giving people what they want that they won't even glance at something that isn't in their "interest area." What a blessing for the people whose only fear in life is negative public opinion about their brand.

It was the Web news sites that did it, back when we were starting out. You remember? That wall between church and state kind of withered away and suddenly you had ad managers deciding what played because it would sell the most ads. And somehow that devolved even further into writing and packaging the paper to sell ads, period.

Which I suppose is how it always was, only now with all this personalization you don't have to see all that boring general interest news; you just get exactly what you want (or what will make you stick around to see more ads, which the feeds have taught us to think of as the same thing). And who can argue with that? "They won't read it anyway, and it will mess up our numbers if we run it," the editors tell me, and you have to give up eventually because it's all about making money for the stockholders—not about creating a responsible news report.

Maybe I'm too old for this. But tell them it's still a hell of a fun job. Just don't let them think they'll be able to change the system. You'd have to do away with publicly traded media companies first, and that will happen sometime after older women are seen as figures of respect.

Talk to you soon,
Anna Wei

Notes

*   Feed—A news collector (like the old AP) that repackages basic story elements for different indies
**   Indie—Free individualized news feeds, determined by viewer usage patterns and designed to keep consumers viewing ads

Elizabeth Weise is a technology writer with USA Today*'s Life section, based in San Francisco. She co-edited* Wired Women: Gender and New Realities in Cyberspace.

Letter from the Future—II

Change is for the better when journalists stop
seeing themselves as victims.

Geneva Overholser

May 1, 2025

DEAR JIM,

I've been thinking back to the end of the '90s, when we were struggling so with journalism's problems: remember how overwhelming they seemed? We felt such gloom—in all those workshops and seminars we sat through together, all aimed at finding a way out of our daunting problems. Isn't it remarkable how much better things turned out than we'd imagined?

I wonder if you'd agree that the key was shrugging off victimhood. We all were feeling so at the mercy of things—of the 24-hour news schedule, of the Net and what was happening to advertising dollars, of tabloidization and corporatization, market supremacy and entertainment as king. You name it, we feared it. But somehow, we started finding leadership in ourselves. We seized the reins—at least where we could—and accommodated more effectively what we had to accept.

Interestingly, the thing that worried me most did take place: the fragmentation, the end of hard-copy newspapers as true mass media—defining, even holding together, large communities. But our comfort in embracing different means of delivery increased so rapidly, and connections *among* all the media increased so richly, that we managed to maintain enormous influence. Once we quit seeing all other media as enemies and began to see ourselves as foundation, connector, even

9

index to others—a nucleus in the multidimensional atom of communication—we found a new vitality.

I was thinking of this last week when the big story on ethnic strife
in Central Africa came to a head. I happened to be in Tampa and
picked up the *Tribune*, which rewarded me with a feast of information
about how to get *more* information so as to understand this difficult
story. Of course, the paper had its own good map and background
basics and a reference to its own interactive Web site as well as
"Tribfacts" fax and audio information. But the paper also highlighted
notices of the president's speech that night, two television specials,
other good Web sites, three substantial magazine explainers now on
newsstands, details about a community interfaith meeting coming up,
addresses for charitable contributions and recent votes of local con-
gressmen on U.S. policy toward Central Africa. In the old days, we
were loathe to acknowledge the existence of other media, much less
steer readers toward them. Now here was the *Tribune* as communications central for Tampa. I wasn't surprised to hear that its newsstand
sales were terrific.

Of course, the costs and benefits of the changes have been inter-
twined. The profit pressures we were under just before the turn of the
millennium—and most newspapers' cautious and fearful response to
them—had so squeezed down our circulation that we weren't really
mass media anyway, most of us. The good news was that this dramatically reduced our costs in newsprint, production, delivery. Some of
our greatest problems—our dull predictability, poor circulation service, price inflexibility—were relieved when we finally embraced the
notion that we were much more than what came off the presses daily.
With Web sites, fax-information delivery, weekly publications with
different circulation bases, greater cooperation with broadcast outlets—
we managed to extend our reach and authority even as we cut our
costs.

Meanwhile, though, we kept the mother ship intact and began again
to strengthen it. Of course, the thing you found most dispiriting—
corporatization—didn't stop. But the top business folks began to understand the threat posed to their own interests by the failure to invest
in training, in salaries, in innovative (but at first financially risky)
ways to reach customers. Hiring stepped up, along with training and
support for investigative reporting and for long-term, comprehensive
projects so important to communities. More knowledgeable beat re-

porting, better writing, even serialization, came back into favor. The change seemed to come quickly, didn't it, once it finally came?

The Monica Lewinsky scandal proved the turning point. What we thought was a drearily endless downhill slide was in fact the outwardmost point of a pendulum swing—one that had started out happily enough. Over the decades before the scandal, we had achieved greater legal protection; we'd loosed ourselves from the suffocatingly close relationship with government. We'd found our footing in great investigative work.

But the trends went too far—well past recovery from one set of excesses, far into their problematic opposites. Watchdogging, a fine advance over collusion with government, had morphed into sneering attack. A welcome skepticism had soured into cynicism. Newspapers known for their vigorous investigative stories became delivery vessels for leaks.

The public unhappiness that had been growing for years came spectacularly to a head after the Clinton impeachment. Just as the public showed sounder judgment than Congress, they showed sounder judgment than the press: there was more to life than this scandal, but media absorption with it sucked the air out of everything else. The public reaction finally came pretty close to rebellion, wouldn't you say?

Remember the Pew Research Center poll right after the impeachment trial? It showed 72 percent of the public saying the media were "propagating scandals." Two-thirds said the press displayed a disregard for the people it covers; the same percentage said it tried to cover up its own mistakes. More than a third called us just plain immoral.

Like an alcoholic hitting bottom, we finally got it. We—journalists and owners alike—realized that our problems weren't someone else's doing, but ours. Our failure to serve readers and customers well, our cheapening of what we did, our desertion of our ethical underpinnings, our finger-wagging sanctimoniousness and generally getting too big for our britches: it had all come back to bite us.

Good papers across the country began to refuse sneering attacks and anonymously sourced stories from Washington. More women and minorities, in more leadership positions, helped shake the arrogance out of our newsrooms. Owners began to understand how we threatened our own First Amendment status when we behaved just like any other business—or worse. It was tough for Wall Street to break its addiction to 25 percent profit margins, but a handful of strong CEOs mustered the courage to call for reinvestment. And public disenchantment with media was so serious that their words carried the day.

Editors began to toss out their well-honed excuses for the worst excesses: "In a digital age, there's little time for contemplation," or, "Everyone else is doing it." The best of them decided to distinguish themselves by differentiating their papers from the pack—by returning to their roots and strengthening their commitment to ethical soundness. Pushed partly by the democratizing influence of the Web, editors began to place accountability and responsiveness to readers in the middle of their enterprises.

We finally ditched the tired old false dichotomy between giving readers what they want and what they need. We reclaimed our civic responsibility to give them what they need, how they want it—appealing and accessible and comprehensive and balanced and fair. We appointed more ombudsmen, organized more *readers* advisory groups. Media criticism—in newspapers and in other publications—increased. State news councils proliferated.

The Web also acted as a strong enforcer of standards. Smart readers could instantly access the speeches and reports from which we worked, or check other sources—and see when our stories lacked balance, when a quote was out of context, when we'd pulled one of our math-phobic blunders. Our tendency to use jargon virtually disappeared, as readers let us know how much they disliked being left out of the loop. Isn't it amazing how our reporting skills tightened up, and what a baseless vanity our refusal to acknowledge error was shown to be? Corrections increased in number and candor. We even began to make them understandable.

The change in attitude toward readers spread throughout good newsrooms. Reporters grew to respect and appreciate the input of readers. We even got over our ignorant dismissal of what we used to see as readers' mindless hankering for good news—and realized that the real problem was our own mindless hankering for conflict, so destructive of civic life and democracy (something you so despaired of our ever understanding). Like so much else, the public got this well before we did.

Don't you think in fact that the very renewal of citizen activity helped cause many issues to resurface in newspapers? The vibrancy of civic life was so strong a repudiation of our dwelling on conflict and pathologies that we finally opened our eyes. Even our color awareness increased: we actually gained the ability to recognize shades of gray—and, of course, to report much more thoughtfully on racial and ethnic issues. Local journalism flourished, focusing on what an issue really meant for readers and how they could get involved. On the other hand, citizen interest also showed up the foolishness of our deserting foreign news just as globalization took hold. Alternative weeklies, meanwhile, led us back to strong investigative work.

Remember civic journalism? It gradually matured, acknowledging that some of its best points had been around long before it coined a name for them and jettisoning some of its most unsettling aspects. But the heart of it, the quest to grow closer to one's community, was widely embraced. (Now, of course, we have today's fad—the League of Citizen Publishers movement.) Meanwhile, the constant shuffling of editors and publishers ceased, reflecting an understanding that the best way to know your community is to live in it—at length.

One of the best developments is the differentiation among newspapers as to ideological and professional makeup and stance. (How amazing to see newspapers proliferating, rather than dwindling as we had expected.) But now we're all much more straightforward about who we are. We have many more media candidly positioned on the left and right, as in Europe. Yet others—the best, generally—have staked their reputations on balance and fairness.

The twist is that these nonaligned newspapers use all manner of different treatments—but with much more forthrightness about what's what. Thus you have straight news stories, interpretation and analysis, much more primary-source material like speeches and reports, and vigorous opinions. But each is clearly labeled and placed in the newspaper—or Web site or whatever—accordingly. Political gossip, anonymously sourced, goes where it belongs—in political gossip columns, not on the front pages where it was appearing in the '90s. And readers are let in on what other media are doing—but in columns designed to do just that. When editors believe a story that played big elsewhere is not up to their standards, they say so—one of the many ways they now speak honestly with readers, explaining inclusions, omissions, tough decisions.

Lord knows we still have plenty of pundits on television—and now on the Internet. But none pretends to be a reporter as well. The public aversion to an anchor or reporter who brought them news one day and pious pronouncements the next finally sank that unappealing practice.

In short, we're all far more honest about ourselves. Our credibility has been restored accordingly. To think back to the 1990s' lame self-justifications for various unjustifiable practices is to wonder how it could have gotten as far as it did.

Other improvements helped, too, of course. Graphics became a completely integral part of our papers at last. Now, information is much more clearly and easily understood—and basic "primer" information can be easily reused, as complex national and international stories unfold.

We're much better at getting our information into classrooms, both hard copy and electronic. And young people quickly began turning to news-media-associated Web sites, once the early infatuation with the great plethora of tidbits available on the Web turned to a hunger for selectivity and credibility.

Still, I'd say the central explanation for our good health lies in the decision by the best journalists to compete for higher ground rather than for a faster-breaking story or more lurid detail. Thank heavens, some editors found their heads and realized they could be proud not to tell a story that was half-baked, *not* to use an anonymous source.

Unsurprisingly, the pleasure in newspapering has resumed. We are attracting a rich and diverse array of talent. With better training, and more hopeful and constructive work, newsrooms are vibrant again. Journalists are respected and—best of all—believed.

We were right to fear our future. But we were wrong to think it would all end badly. Daily journalism in 2025 is serving this democracy's needs better than it has at any time since you and I spiked our first copy in 1970. And best of all, we no longer have to endure those endless throes of self-examination.

Yours in hope,
Geneva

Geneva Overholser, a syndicated columnist, is the former editor of The Des Moines Register *and former ombudsman for* The Washington Post.

The Future Is the Net

News on-line is here to stay.

Jon Katz

TIME IS GETTING a little short for mainstream journalism—by which I mean newspapers, magazines and broadcast news—to decide whether they want to completely alienate younger consumers or not.

The Internet is just beginning to grow as opposed to being a fad that will disappear. The Web is transforming culture, it is transforming language, transforming information, and we're seeing this in very dramatic and measurable ways, which some liken to the invention of movable type.

Journalism is still looking at the Internet and asking if this is a good witch or a bad witch, but the debate has gone to another point and the culture has grown so rapidly beyond that question. The Web is the central reality—economic, social, cultural, political—for younger generations, whether we like it or not, whether we think it is a good thing or not. I don't think the Web is supplanting culture; it is creating new culture.

The number of people of younger generations who are consuming mainstream journalism is really getting fractional, and it's a shame that this group is being so ignored by journalism as it is the most powerful group in the country. They are not used to ever consuming news in the passive manner of older generations. They have no tradition of reading a magazine or a newspaper from front to back or of watching the evening news from beginning to end. And while they gather information through a variety of sources, they do care about

15

issues and will read things they are interested in. Their agenda, however, is very different. Fifty-five million people read the Starr report on-line in some form or another and then quickly left the story behind after coming to the conclusion that Clinton would survive. While it was the central story in journalism for months, the on-line public made it clear that they do not care about Monica Lewinsky, that they were not reading that story and they did not think journalism should be covering it.

The model of a few people dispensing information to many is breaking down, and now many people are dispensing information to many people. This is a potentially dangerous situation. But when a story breaks, Americans do not go to Web sites we have never heard of—they go quickly to sites we have heard of. The No. 1 site for news on the Web is CNN, followed by *USA Today*, followed by ABC News. The major news sites on the Web are all traditional names, which is great news for journalism if it would embrace it, accept it and capitalize off of it.

There need to be gatekeepers of information, but there also needs to be a willingness to share power. The on-line culture is about a willingness to alter the relationship between the vendor and the consumer of information. People who grow up in this interactive culture take this relationship as a right, not as a privilege. They control the information they use, and they do it through technology. This is not a question of good or bad; it is just the truth. And I think if we want to survive as an institution we must communicate with younger generations. Journalism needs to move beyond this clucking about whether this is a horrible thing or not and be much more innovative in covering it.

All the rules are being rewritten. It is unlike anything we have seen before. Ask any news media executive, and he'll tell you that the industry is never going to be the same. The demographics show that people are not returning to traditional sources of information, and the attitude that throughout history this has happened before is wrong. This idea of who owns intellectual property and how it is distributed is really going to change. And it's more important that the news media understand it and explain it to the people than it is that we simply reflexively condemn and attack.

There is a disconnect—the country is going one way and journalism is going another. It is getting pretty alarming for someone who likes journalism as I do. I am distressed that journalists are not really as into this as they need to be for their own survival. When I talk about whether journalism will survive, I think of it as a prodding instinct, not as a wish. Journalism really needs to survive, especially in this age where there is so much information from so many different places. It is raining down on our heads, and we have no way of knowing how to evaluate it. Whenever have we needed a more coherent source of information than now—people we can trust, people who understand how to gather facts, people who know how to present them coherently?

Jon Katz, a media critic, is a contributing editor to Rolling Stone *and* slashdot.org. *He is the author of several books, including* Virtuous Reality. *His comments are adapted from remarks delivered at a fellows' seminar given at the Media Studies Center on March 18, 1999.*

Lawyers, Voyeurs, and Vigilantes

*Journalists and our democratic institutions are
in a dangerously deformed relationship.*

James W. Carey

I BEGIN FROM a simple but strangely controversial assumption: journalism and democracy share a common fate. No journalism, no democracy. What journalist would disagree? But journalists are less likely to agree with its equally true obverse: without democracy there can be no journalism. When democracy falters, journalism falters and when journalism goes awry, democracy goes awry.

The assumption is controversial, for it seems to commit journalists to the defense of something, to compromise their valued independence or nonpartisanship. It claims that journalists can be independent or objective about everything but democracy, for to do so is to abandon the craft. About democratic institutions, about the way of life of democracy, journalists are not permitted to be indifferent, nonpartisan or objective. It is their one compulsory passion, for it forms the ground condition of their practice. Without the institutions or spirit of democracy, journalists are reduced to propagandists or entertainers. The passion for democracy is the one necessary bond journalists must have with the public—which they misleadlingly call and demean as their audience or market.

The assumption is easily supported by the history of totalitarianism in the 20th century. American journalists pretty much universally agreed that while there were people in the old Soviet Union who called themselves journalists, who worked for things called newspapers, broadcast

19

stations and magazines, such people were not journalists but propagandists. Their organizations did not constitute a press but the apparatus of a state and a party. Soviet journalism was an oxymoron—without the institutions of democracy, including freedom of expression protected by law or tradition, it was a sham.

But journalism can be destroyed by forces other than the totalitarian state; it can also be destroyed by the entertainment state. When journalists measure their success solely by the size of their readership or audience, by the profits of their companies or by their incomes, status and visibility, they have caved into the temptation of worshipping false gods, of selling their heritage for a pottage—just as much as those who cynically convinced themselves they were serving democracy by acting as the mouthpieces of a putatively revolutionary party.

This is the caution we need as we move forward from the Lewinsky/Clinton scandal. In the aftermath of the impeachment process, most notably following Barbara Walters' cynical interview with Ms. Lewinsky, it was proclaimed that the "system worked"; the press had played its historical role. It was the same as the proclamations issued, with much more justification, when Richard Nixon waved goodbye to us from the steps of the military helicopter perched on the lawn of the White House. But what such self-congratulatory pronouncements miss is an understanding of the depth of the historical process in which journalists and democratic institutions are enmeshed and the dangers present in what is currently a deformed relationship.

I BELIEVE A VIRUS has infected the American body politic and journalists are not immune to it. We know approximately when and where it was introduced—Washington, between John Kennedy's assassination and Richard Nixon's resignation—but we do not know how to rid ourselves of the contamination. Our political institutions have been in a slow-motion free-fall for a couple of decades, their authority, vitality and credibility slowly being eroded. A strong presidency, an independent judiciary, a self-governing congress and a free press are our most precious institutions, and I cannot imagine a way of life without them. The republican ideals embedded in these institutions provide the foundation for a democratic state and free public life.

The actors who drove the impeachment process and the scandals that ignited and sustained it—lawyers with contempt for the law, journalists reveling in voyeurism, and political vigilantes and opportunists, including the president, ready to indulge and profit from any dishonor—seem no longer to understand this nor to hold the republic in their imaginations. Their landscape comprises more the human body than the body politic. The cultural reality within which they unfolded this story was an adult theme park fabricated by Disney types. They created new sites for prurience and indignation, but not for democratic politics.

As a result our institutions continue to interact in a whirlpool of mutual degradation, one that resembles a "behavioral sink," threatening to drag us all down. As the same technological system comes to underlie all our institutions, they become entrapped in a system of high-speed interaction, the barriers between them eroded, running on nanosecond timetables that threaten both their stability and legitimacy.

I believe, on intuition alone, that these understandings were widely shared if dimly grasped by the American people and, as a result, they resisted mightily the further erosion of the presidency when everyone else seemed committed only to degrading it. The public understood that the presidency is the principal symbolic and administrative institution of our political life. Moreover, they sensed what politicians and journalists seem to have forgotten. It was a central belief of the Founding Fathers, based on the experience of history, that republican institutions are fragile, the moments of their existence fleeting in historical time—some 200 years on average they thought—and we had to guard against lurching back into a life of domination. We now seem to take these institutions for granted as if they are indestructible. Journalists seem to believe that democratic politics, which alone underwrites their craft, is a self-perpetuating machine that will run of itself, that can withstand any amount of undermining. Nothing is further from the truth.

I am not suggesting that we are living in an imaginative proximity to revolution. Americans love change but hate revolution, the exact opposite of the French. But revolution is not the only option open to people in this wealthy society. People can also retreat deeper into private life, inside gated communities, seeking private solutions to public problems, consigning politics to the realm of game and spectacle for mass distraction, a place inhabited by cretins governed by the lowest of motives. But who is hurt by this? The weakest and most vulnerable among us, which is why so many clung to the presidency in the midst of a general revulsion. "Nations are the skin of the poor," the

Latin American economist Hernando De Soto says, understanding that nations are most precious to those orphaned and defenseless.

DEMOCRATIC INSTITUTIONS will survive this president and special prosecutor. The system may have worked after a fashion, but that is not inevitable. The increased speed of interaction among these institutions has it own multiplier effect. One day they could spin wildly out of control. The best we can hope for now is that the whirlpool will bottom out with this episode, and we can begin the task of reconstructing democratic institutions, including the press. That is the urgent task. What is more likely, however, is that Bill Clinton's, Kenneth Starr's and the House manager's supporters, aflame with vengeance, will lie in wait for the next president and political hysteria will start all over again. Let us remind them of the old adage I once heard in Ireland: vengeance is a dish best eaten cold.

In the last 35 years we have shot one president out of office (and tried to assassinate two others), forced another not to run for re-election, compelled one to resign, had two serve unsuccessful first terms and denied them re-election, and had a two year presidency for an unelected vice-president. Not a record of stability in our highest office. Ronald Reagan, the exception in this chronology, was on the ropes during a deep constitutional crisis involving the central doctrine of separation of powers, but we pulled back from the logical outcome. Now Clinton will limp to the end of his second term, damaged by his own recklessness to be sure, and by the reckless disregard of democratic politics indulged by friends, enemies and journalists alike.

There is a deep irony here. We came through the Great Depression and World War II with our institutions relatively unscathed, never really afflicted by the temptations of authoritarianism and totalitarianism. As a result, democracy could sum up the dreams of revolutionaries in Eastern Europe and elsewhere. Journalist Timothy Garton Ash tells us "that the leaders of the revolutions ... had a startlingly clear idea of the constitutional order they wanted to build which bore not a little resemblance" to that fostered by the American revolution. Observing this last episode in American politics with nonplussed apprehension, they must now feel they are being integrated into a burning house, for as they join the community of democratic nations, we act as if we are leaving it.

That is the background of our recent political trauma. One should not take consolation by comparing it to the deeper crisis of Watergate. Much has changed. The judiciary was a benign and sober guide through that crisis. It has been at the center of this one following a series of "scandals"—O.J., Robert Bork, Clarence Thomas and Anita Hill, to put names to them—which have deeply undermined the integrity of that institution. The damage done to the oft-proclaimed rule of law by the special proscecutor and his staff, along with his collaborators in the press, has deepened suspicions of citizens about the rectitude of our courts. Congress and the press have suffered parallel declines in public trust and esteem. The "new media" have quickened the cycles of interaction. The 24-hour news cycle is now a 22-minute one and, as a result, we moved from an initial report to discussions of impeachment within a working day or two. Indeed, outbreaks of these scandals are now partly a function of unused capacity in communications: too much time and space chasing too little information. As a result, news is displaced by hyperbole, rumor and innuendo as if the technology had caused a cultural stroke. And in the midst of this, journalists, particularly on television, seemed to derive unusual pleasure from the national trauma suggesting they no longer have a stake in the republic. After all, if it is good for journalists, it ought to be good for the country.

WHEN ONE ARGUES that the political process itself, and the role of the press within it, is eroding the basis of democratic life, three defenses are rushed in. First, we are told that scandal and calumny are persistent features of our history, that all presidents have been subjected to it going back to Washington and Jefferson. Everything is therefore normal. This overlooks an obvious fact: both American politics and the American press were at one time organized on a partisan basis. Until this century, journalists were either in the employ of political parties or fundamentally aligned with them, and their responsibility was to represent partisan interests. Free competition among those interests would sort out the truth or, failing that, permit the distribution of political loyalties.

With the rise of the independent voter and an independent press, there was a reaction against partisanship in politics and the press. The task of journalism was to stand outside this process, to sort rival claims, to be skeptical about all participants and to produce a more or less truthful record concerning the issues and personalities in contention.

That is the meaning of an independent press; its only loyalty is to the democratic process itself.

That is hardly the case these days. As competition among political interests is always uneven, the press is increasingly controlled at any given point by whoever is in control of the story: at one moment the president, another the special prosecutor, at another whatever unidentified puppeteer is pulling the strings of politics. Skepticism seems to desert journalists, and they are ready to believe anyone, or at least to repeat what anyone says for whatever reason under whatever circumstance. The result is both mass confusion and mass cynicism.

The second defense is to blame it on the American people. "Just look at readership and ratings. We're giving the people what they want no matter how debased their taste." This is a peculiar defense. Journalists first announce that "the presidency is in crisis," which means the country is in crisis. They assume the alert attentiveness of a full national emergency and then feign surprise when people actually tune in, watch and read as if a genuine crisis is in tow. But it is the press that was in crisis, not the body politic. But even this is overstated. Watching television and reading newspapers and magazines are daily habits. A so-called crisis produces marginal changes in those habits, nothing spectacular, yet such changes are trumpeted as a defense. But if CNN's average ratings double, that means they go from .5 to 1.0, 334,000 to 668,000 households. That is a commercially important change—which is one of the problems—but it may not be a politically significant one, particularly as we do not know how self-canceling the increase is: a rise in CNN's audience being mirrored by marginal, and almost imperceptible, declines throughout what is now a vast channel system. This is important in understanding the enormous size of the public for the Walters/Lewinsky interview. Not only was it self-canceling but, more importantly, the size was justified, for it was staged as the final act in a national drama into which the public was deliberately sutured as a Greek chorus. Citizens watched despite their revulsion at all the parties.

But the basic defense of the press is simply that "the devil made us do it. We are victims of the new high-speed competition in communications." True enough. But that merely locates the problem. In our time the First Amendment has ceased to have the implication of a public trust held by the press in the name of a wider community. Rather, it increasingly refers to a mere property right establishing ground rules for economic competition. From a political right it is being converted to an exclusively economic one, and democracy comes to mean solely economic liberty. Lest you think this hyperbolic, listen to Rupert Murdoch, one of the new barons of the conglomerates, who sought and was granted U.S. citizenship solely to increase competition:

> Singapore is not liberal but clean and free of drug addicts. Not so long ago it was an impoverished, exploited colony with famine, diseases, and other problems. Now people find themselves in three-room apartments, with jobs and clean streets. Countries like Singapore are going the right way: material incentives create business and the free market economy as well as perhaps a middle class and with it democracy. If politicians try it the other way around with immediate democracy, the Russian model is the result. 90 per cent of the Chinese are more interested in a better material life than in the right to vote.

WHILE THE ECONOMIC world prizes efficiency, it has less patience for political freedom and democracy. Whereas the triumph of democracy is everywhere heralded, the commitment to actual democracy everywhere has weakened, or, more precisely, our imagination of democracy has shrunk and is equated solely with a limited aspect of even economic democracy: the existence of free and open markets. This is true not only among the public, who it is rather too easy to blame, but even more among privileged classes, including journalists.

But political democracy does not follow from the presence of an effective market economy, and a politically free press does not follow from an economically free one. Indeed, when economic values come to dominate politics, liberty is often at risk. One does not have to believe in conspiracies to observe that economic interests can profit from a weakened nation state. In the absence of global political institutions, only nations are strong enough to contain economic forces. We are learning that the new economism can be quite illiberal. As Murdoch attests, modern economic developments seem to favor authoritarian rather than democratic regimes. Ralf Dahrendorf reminds us that "authoritarian does not mean totalitarian" for, as he says, such regimes do not "require a Great Leader" nor an invasive ideology nor permanent mobilization. Nor do they require a self-perpetuating public class unwilling to relinquish power. Authoritarian countries can be quite nice for the visitor as well as predictable and undemanding for the native. For the poet and the journalist, and many others, they are unbearable—though paradoxically they can produce great literature and journalism if only as acts of protest, a way of learning, in the wonderful phrase of the Polish dissenter Stanislaw Baranczak, to "breathe under water."

The indifference or tolerance of the erosion of democratic institutions, including the press, is predicated on a belief that times will always be good. However, when the economic going gets rough, as it will again, people begin to doubt the constitution of liberty and embrace illiberal political projects. In such a crisis it might prove impossible to reinvent and repair institutions we have so carelessly damaged.

THE ULTIMATE JUSTIFICATION for journalism and the First Amendment is that together they constitute us as a civil society and set us in conversation with one another. Journalism is our public diary, our day book, and as such it forms our collective memory. Republics are structures of memory, and, as Milan Kundera says at the opening of *The Book of Laughter and Forgetting*, "the struggle of man against power is the struggle of memory against forgetting." But as one crisis succeeds another in the United States of Amnesia, each becomes eminently forgettable, though each leaves a trace, an image—one eighth grader interviewed on television could only remember the "semen on a dress"—on the national unconscious. Because fiction, history, comedy and conversation are happy parasites on journalism—they begin from the news of the day—these destructive images are what remain in public memory. These are not good images to carelessly implant in public memory. The best injunction for journalists to keep in mind for the future is Sir Walter Scott's: it's not fish you're buying; it's men's and women's lives.

James W. Carey, a 1985 Media Studies Center inaugural fellow, is a professor at Columbia University's Graduate School of Journalism. He is author of Communication as Culture: Essays on Media and Society.

Who?

*Diversity in journalism is not a feel-good exercise.
It is essential if reporters are to achieve the accuracy
that journalism demands.*—FARAI CHIDEYA

Who Will Be Journalists
in the Next Century?

More women, more people of color, fewer Protestants,
more young people, more Democrats

David Weaver

THE OCCUPATION OF journalist in the United States has been vaguely defined from the early days of the republic. During the 1700s to the mid-1800s, American journalism was basically an apprenticeship system where aspiring novices such as Benjamin Franklin learned the trade in print shops, and where the role of journalist was fulfilled largely by the town printer and correspondent. By the middle of the 19th century, as American society became more complex and many of its journalistic operations resembled corporate enterprises, the term journalist came to describe reporters, writers, correspondents, columnists, newsmen (and a few women) and editors who worked mainly for newspapers and magazines. In the 20th century, this term was broadened to include radio and television news announcers, reporters, editors and even some on-line computer writers and editors.

Who will journalists likely be in the next century and millennium? This article speculates on that question by examining the most comprehensive surveys of U.S. journalists done in this century, surveys that focus on journalists' formal educational experiences, gender, racial and ethnic origins, age, political leanings and religious backgrounds.

IN HIS TRAVELS throughout the America of 1831, French writer-politician Alexis de Tocqueville was impressed that almost every hamlet had a newspaper. But the printers who produced these sheets were "generally in very humble position with a scanty education and vulgar turn of mind" according to de Tocqueville, with "open and coarse appeals to the passions of their readers." In 1833, a young job printer named Benjamin Day began *The Sun* in New York by selling copies on the street for a penny instead of the usual 6-cent subscription price. The occupation of reporter began to emerge with Day's hiring of veteran London police writer George Wisner. As sociologist Michael Schudson has written, the idea of paying reporters "was not only novel, but to some, shocking. Until the late 1820s, New York coverage of Washington politics relied mainly on members of Congress writing occasionally to their home papers." By 1834, two of New York's 11 papers each employed four reporters to obtain the "earliest, fullest, and most correct intelligence on every local incident," wrote journalism historian Willard Bleyer, quoting the editor of the New York *Evening Transcript.*

But the occupation of hired reporter was not accorded instant respect, and some journalists would argue (proudly at times) that it never has reached very high levels of esteem in this country. Nevertheless, by the time Joseph Pulitzer had moved east to buy *The New York World* in 1883, journalism historian Frank Luther Mott notes that reporters were getting frequent bylines, especially in Sunday editions, and that those in the larger cities tended to be formally educated and to draw salaries comparable to those of city editors.

Whereas the occupation of journalist in the United States had been almost exclusively populated by men for more than a century, women began to make inroads into journalism during the 1880s. *The Journalist* of New York, one of the first trade publications in the field, estimated that some 500 women worked on the editorial side of American newspapers during this period, and that 200 of them were on New York newspapers. Women's press clubs were organized at the local level, and a Women's International Press Association was founded in 1885.

By the late 1800s, some U.S. journalists were characterizing their work as something more than a mere trade, perhaps because of a desire for more social respectability as well as a yearning for higher standards of truth and accuracy after the excesses of the Yellow Journalism period in which sensationalistic reporting was common. Whitelaw Reid, editor and publisher of *The New York Tribune,* told a meeting of the newly formed Ohio Press Association in 1879 that journalism was now a profession. Some quickly disagreed with that assessment, including *The Nation*, an elite journal of commentary, arguing that journalism was a commercial field that required no special education. Half a century later, in 1947, the Hutchins Commission on Freedom of the Press disagreed, recommending that journalists be better educated to be able to place the facts in a context that gave them meaning.

PERHAPS THE FIRST systematic study of U.S. journalists was done by Leo Rosten when he surveyed Washington reporters in 1936. He found that half were college graduates, a figure that rose to 81 percent in William Rivers' 1961 study and to 93 percent in Stephen Hess' 1978 study, far above the overall population figure of about one-sixth. A follow-up survey of the White House press corps by Hess in 1991 found 95 percent with college degrees, and a 1992 survey by Hess of some 400 foreign correspondents working for U.S. news organizations found 98 percent with an undergraduate degree.

The first large-scale national survey of all U.S. journalists, done in 1971 by University of Illinois at Chicago sociologist John Johnstone and his doctoral students Edward Slawski and William Bowman, found nearly 60 percent were college graduates. Two later national surveys by this author and G. Cleveland Wilhoit of Indiana University found this figure rising to nearly 75 percent in 1982 and 82 percent in 1992, a clear indication that the four-year bachelor's degree was becoming the minimum qualification for a full-time job as a journalist in mainstream general interest U.S. news media. This is a trend that seems to be irreversible, especially in newsmagazines, news services, daily newspapers and television.

Whether this trend will extend to graduate degrees is questionable. The 1971 survey found 7 percent with graduate degrees, but this proportion increased only slightly to 11 percent in 1982 and remained the same for 1992, suggesting no trend of increases in graduate degree holders among U.S. journalists in general. Among Washington reporters, however, there was an upward trend from 6 percent in 1936 to 20 percent in 1961 to 33 percent in 1978 who had earned graduate degrees. This trend seems evident among U.S. newsmagazine journalists as well, with 31 percent of them holding graduate degrees in 1992, far more than any other kind of journalist in this national survey of more than 1,100. Among foreign correspondents, an even higher percentage (40 percent) had earned graduate degrees according to Hess' 1992 survey.

In short, the more elite U.S. journalists are more likely than other journalists to have graduate degrees, a trend that seems likely to become more pronounced over time, but these degrees are not necessarily in journalism. In the 1978 survey of Washington reporters, 48 percent earned their graduate degrees in journalism, a figure that dropped to 39 percent in 1991. And among foreign correspondents in 1992, only 18 percent majored in journalism at the undergraduate level and 38 percent at the graduate level. The most common majors of those not concentrating on journalism were in the humanities and liberal arts; only 3 percent at the undergraduate level and 6 percent at the graduate level had majors in science or technical fields.

But over time, the percentage of journalism majors seems likely to increase in U.S. news media in general. A recent study by Lee Becker of the University of Georgia found 75 percent of entry-level hires in daily newspapers coming from journalism-mass communication college programs, and the 1992 Weaver-Wilhoit survey indicated that 68 percent of those journalists under 25 had majored in journalism or mass communication in college. Even among those journalists with graduate degrees, the 1992 national survey found a significant increase in the percentage majoring in journalism and mass communication from about half in 1982 to nearly 60 percent in 1992.

ALONG WITH AN increase in the proportions of journalists studying journalism and mass communication in college is likely to come an increase in women journalists. Recent studies of U.S. journalism school enrollments by Lee Becker of the University of Georgia and Jerry Kosicki of Ohio State University show 61 percent women enrolled and 60 percent of the bachelor's degrees going to women in journalism-mass communication programs throughout the country. The 1992 Weaver-Wilhoit national survey of U.S. journalists shows no increase from 1982 in women journalists throughout all print and broadcast news media (34 percent), but a notably higher percentage of women among those journalists with fewer than five years' experience (45 percent), under 25 years of age (49 percent), and those working in weekly newspapers (44 percent) or newsmagazines (46 percent).

Among the more elite Washington journalists, the percentage of women was only 21 in 1978, but that increased substantially to 31 percent in Hess' 1991 study, suggesting an upward trend. Likewise, retired Ohio University journalism professor Ralph Kliesch's studies of American media correspondents reporting from abroad show an increase in women from 10 percent in 1975 to 25 percent in 1990, and Hess' 1992 survey of foreign correspondents finds 29 percent women.

If most women choose to stay in journalism, their overall proportions should increase substantially in the next century. That is questionable, however, given past patterns that suggest more rapid defection of women than men from the journalistic ranks. Except for weekly newspapers and newsmagazines, it may be that the overall proportion of women in U.S. journalism will not rise much above the one-third mark in the foreseeable future, in spite of their majorities in most journalism schools.

The proportion of women journalists in the 1992 Weaver-Wilhoit national survey varied considerably by race, with all minority groups (especially Asians, blacks and Hispanics) represented by more women than the white majority group. This suggests that increased emphasis on hiring minority journalists is likely to increase the representation of women at the same time.

The employment of racial and ethnic minorities in U.S. journalism, despite variations within different media, has not kept up with the employment of women or with the increases of various racial and ethnic groups in the overall population, however. There was some increase during the decade from 1982 to 1992, from about 4 percent to about 8 percent, but this percentage for 1992 still lagged far behind the 24 percent overall non-Caucasian population estimated by the 1990 U.S. Census. In fairness, the proportion of minorities with a bachelor's degree or more—which has become the standard qualification for entry level positions in journalism—was only about 9 percent in 1992, compared with more than twice that percentage among majority whites, as Hess has noted.

As WITH WOMEN, if only those journalists hired during the decade of the 1980s are considered, the overall percentage of minorities was considerably higher (about 12 percent), suggesting that there were increased efforts, and some success, in minority hiring during the 1980s. But the percentage dropped off sharply for those journalists with 10 or more years of experience, probably because of less emphasis on minority hiring during the 1960s and '70s, and possibly because more minorities left journalism after 10 years on the job.

Some media did better than others in recruiting full-time minority journalists, most notably radio (14 percent) and television (12 percent), and some have done much worse. It is likely that the very low percentage of minorities working on weekly newspapers in 1992 (2 percent) reflects the fact that many minorities lived in larger urban areas, but the same cannot be said for newsmagazines (5 percent) and wire services (5 percent).

In 1992, African Americans were the most numerous minority journalists, whereas Native Americans were the least common. When these percentages were projected to the total population of mainstream news media, Weaver and Wilhoit estimated about 4,500 black journalists, 2,700 Hispanics, 1,200 Asians and only 730 Native Americans. It should be remembered that these projections did not include special interest or ethnic media, or any non-newsmagazines, so they were very conservative numbers.

The more elite journalists were even less likely to come from minority ethnic and racial backgrounds, including 6 percent of foreign correspondents in 1992, 5 percent of White House reporters in 1991 and 5 percent of newsmagazine journalists in 1992. There was a slight increase in minorities among Washington journalists, from 3.6 percent in 1978 to 5 percent in 1991, and there was an increase in minority journalists working for daily newspapers in the United States from 6 percent in 1988 to 11.5 percent in 1998, as indicated by the American Society of Newspaper Editors (ASNE) national surveys.

Although there were some real gains in the proportions of minority journalists working in U.S. news media from the early 1980s to the 1990s, these increases were smaller than many would have liked, and some indicators suggest that it may be difficult to retain many of the brightest and most ambitious for very long, given limited opportunities for advancement in a field that has not grown much during this time. Substantial increases in minority journalists in U.S. mainstream news media seem likely only if there are opportunities for advancement and increased responsibilities.

Another trend in American journalism in the past two decades was the aging of journalists. The median age of U.S. journalists rose to 36 years old in 1992, about where it was in 1971, from a drop to almost

32 in 1982. This was especially true for print journalists, with a median age of 37, compared to broadcast, where it was only 32. Ages rose slightly for foreign correspondents (mean age of 43), White House correspondents in 1991 (42) and newsmagazine journalists (40).

This aging of American journalists is even more dramatically illustrated by looking at the proportions in each group. Those under 24 years old shrunk to only about 4 percent of all journalists, down dramatically from nearly 12 percent in both 1971 and 1982, mainly because of the small growth in the number of new jobs during the 1980s. Those 25-34 years old also declined from 45 percent to 37 percent, and those 35-54 grew the most (from 32 to 51 percent), becoming the largest age segment in American journalism in 1992. At the same time, those 55 to 64 years old continued to decline since 1971, suggesting relatively fewer "elders" in American journalism in 1992 as compared with the early 1970s.

Whether this pattern will change much in the next decade as many of those in the large 35-54 group exceed 55 depends on how many stay in journalism and how many move on to other occupations or retire. We do know from the 1992 survey that 21 percent of all journalists said they would like to be working outside the news media in five years, compared to 11 percent in 1982-83 and only 7 percent in 1971. And with many of the baby boomers set to retire in the next decade, it seems likely that there may be another hiring boom, pushing the average age of U.S. journalists down again and providing more opportunities for women and minorities to be hired and to advance in U.S. news media, assuming that the number of full-time jobs remains relatively constant. This assumption is questionable, however, given recent trends in downsizing in many news organizations.

IF MORE WOMEN and minorities are hired by U.S. news media in the next century, this has implications for the future political leanings of journalists. As early as 1936, Leo Rosten found in his survey of Washington correspondents that they were more Democratic and less Republican than the nation as a whole, but Johnstone and his colleagues found in 1971 that U.S. journalists in general were a bit more likely to claim to be Independents than the overall adult population and a bit less likely to identify with either the Democratic or Republican parties, a finding replicated by Weaver and Wilhoit in 1982. By 1992, however, U.S. journalists were substantially more likely to claim to be

Democrats (44 percent) than the country as a whole (34 percent) and notably less likely to consider themselves Republicans (16 percent) than the general population (33 percent).

This trend was especially notable in 1992 among women (58 percent Democrats) and various minority journalists (63 percent Democrats among Asians, 70 percent among African Americans, 59 percent among Hispanics and 52 percent among Native Americans). Likewise, most minority journalists were much less likely to identify with the Republican Party than were majority whites (5 percent of Asians, 1 percent of blacks, 15 percent of Hispanics and 5 percent of Native Americans). Some of these differences could be due partly to the younger average ages of minority journalists, but in most cases the differences are so large that they cannot be explained by age alone. Thus it appears that more hiring of women and minorities will tilt the balance in newsrooms even further toward reporters identifying with the Democratic Party, although this does not mean that news coverage of politics will necessarily favor Democratic politicians or policies, given reputable news organizations' standards of fairness and accuracy, the professional norms of journalism and commercial constraints.

Another difference between minority and majority journalists is in religious backgrounds. Whereas the religion of U.S. journalists in general has closely matched the overall U.S. population percentages of Protestant, Catholic and Jewish from 1971 to 1992 (with a slight overrepresentation of Jewish and a slight underrepresentation of other or no religion), this is not the case for many minority journalists. For example, Asians, Hispanics and Native Americans were significantly less likely to come from Protestant backgrounds (15 to 35 percent) than were whites (55 percent); African Americans were more likely to (67 percent). Not surprisingly, Hispanic journalists were much more likely to come from Catholic religious backgrounds (82 percent) than whites (30 percent) and all other groups (14 to 23 percent).

Minorities in general were notably less likely to come from a Jewish background (0 to 1 percent) than white majority journalists (6 percent). Asian journalists were especially likely to claim no religious background (29 percent) as compared with whites (5 percent) and other minorities (1 to 7 percent), and Native American journalists were most likely to come from a religious background other than those mentioned above (37 percent vs. 4 percent for whites, 12 percent for Asians and 14 percent African Americans).

IN 1992, THIS author and G. Cleveland Wilhoit concluded that the "typical" U.S. journalist was a white Protestant male with a bachelor's degree from a public college, married, 36 years old, earning about $31,000 a year, working in journalism about 12 years, not belonging to a journalism association and employed by a medium-sized group-owned daily newspaper.

It seems likely, from the trends reviewed here, that this portrait will change substantially in the next century in the direction of more color, less maleness, less Protestantism (especially among the growing corps of Hispanic journalists), a younger average age and more identification with the Democratic Party and more liberal political views. It also seems likely that the average salary will increase, but it is less clear as to whether more journalists will belong to professional associations (although minority journalists were considerably more likely to in 1992) and whether the majority of U.S. journalists will continue to work for daily newspapers, given the rise of new on-line and broadcast media.

One thing seems clear from these trends—the journalists of the next century will be more representative of the larger U.S. society demographically than those of this past century. They will also be more formally educated and more inclined to be independent thinkers who cannot be easily duped or manipulated. Whether most of them will work for traditional news organizations, however, is less clear, given the development of Web zines and other on-line publications, as well as other opportunities in the growing fields of corporate communication and public relations.

The challenge for traditional news media will be to provide the resources and the support for the best and the brightest, so that they are not tempted to stray from serious journalism. In this postmodern age when so many boundaries are blurring, including those between fact and fiction, this is a serious challenge for journalism and for the larger society.

David Weaver is the Roy W. Howard Research Professor at Indiana University's School of Journalism. He has worked as a newspaper journalist and has published nine books on journalists, polls and the role of the media in politics, including The American Journalist *and* The Global Journalist.

Who's a Journalist?—I

The answer lies in training, character and attitude.

Ted Gup

JOURNALISM, IT WAS said by one eminent practitioner, was once "a craft to be mastered in four days, and abandoned at the first sign of a better job." That was H.L. Mencken. Half a century ago he made sport of journalism's pretensions and those who sought to "inject plausible theories into its practice, and rid it of its old casualness and opportunism." Journalism, a profession? Mencken scoffed at the idea. Lawyers and doctors, he observed, could regulate and license those who practiced their professions. The journalist, he noted, "is unable, as yet, to control admission to his craft."

Never was that truer than today. Virtually anyone appearing in print, on cable or with access to a computer and a modem may present himself or herself to the world as a journalist. No longer is there even a pretense that journalists control admission to the craft, something Mencken viewed as the hallmark of a true profession. To many, today's developments and tomorrow's promise are cause for celebration. The old barriers to entry into the field—capital and the clubbiness of the Old Boy Network—are being dismantled. The hoi polloi, say its proponents, are empowered to speak and to be heard. With the advent of the Internet, the expansion of cable and other technologies, we are witness to a revolution, a universal enfranchisement in which suddenly everyone is a journalist. I am not so sure.

While there may be much to celebrate in these developments and what they portend for the future, there is also much to cause concern, particularly when it comes to journalism. Call me old-fashioned, but I believe that there is more to being a journalist than simply being heard. A thousand people may take up the microphone in *karaoke*, and yet not one of them may be a singer. It is a fallacy that everyone may be a journalist—as if the title were conferred along with the capability to project one's voice, one's image or one's words.

WHO IS A JOURNALIST? Some will say that the question is elitist, that it comes from a profession intent upon protecting its franchise, like some medieval guild that awakens to discover history has passed it by. "All professions are conspiracies against the laity," observed George Bernard Shaw. But there is nothing elitist or anti-democratic about believing that the public is entitled to the very best information, that it benefits from trained observers who understand not only the demands of meeting deadlines, but also the virtues of restraint, of confirmation, of accuracy, balance and fairness.

Who is a journalist? The question becomes even more critical in an age filled with a multiplicity of unrecognizable voices and a torrent of information that strains our ability to hear any one voice. More and more people are speaking. Their words are arriving faster and faster. It may well be democracy in action, but it is also confusing. What was needed at the Tower of Babel was not another voice but a trained interpreter.

Who is a journalist? A person who may help us to decipher between those whom we wish to hear and heed and those who are merely purveyors of rumor, gossip, intrigue, propaganda, disinformation and all manner of other mischief. The question today, as before, goes to the heart of who is worthy of public trust and cognizant of the special responsibilities that go along with that trust. Not all voices are equal. The notion of egalitarianism is not based on the idea that human beings are fungible assets, readily interchangeable, but rather that all should be given equal opportunity to demonstrate their acquired skills and intrinsic character.

Traditionally there have been many ways for journalists to garner the sort of bona fides that persuaded others that they were indeed journalists. For some it was formal academic training at prestigious universities like Northwestern, Missouri or Columbia. Others might point to some credentialing process, as if a laminated press pass around the neck was evidence that one is a journalist. Still others would say that it is by dint of affiliation. Who would argue that someone from CBS, *The New York Times* or *Time* magazine was not a journalist? But in truth, all such criteria are superficial, merely the trappings of the profession and not the profession itself. At least as many journalistic sins have been committed under a Hearst or Luce or Murdoch masthead, or by graduates of fine universities, as by the unaffiliated, uneducated and unknown.

Indeed, the public's suspicions of the profession and their rancor is often directed to the very core of those reporters with the most prestigious credentials. They sense that these journalists have become too comfortable, that they identify with those in power whom they cover, that they are driven by ego and not service or have been co-opted by the corporate giants for whom they work. Yet journalism has always been at its best when its ranks are filled with independent outsiders— be it ideological (think I.F. Stone, A.J. Liebling, Seymour Hersh) or geographical, like the legion of small-town Midwesterners and Southerners who come to the newsrooms of New York, Washington, Los Angeles and places in between, bringing with them a skeptic's eye and a foreigner's perspective. There is no requisite pedigree to practicing the craft, nothing more than a reverence for the work and a willingness to acquire the skills to serve.

Who then is a journalist? The answer lies in the sum of training, character and attitude. Of the three, perhaps training—the conveyance of basic journalistic skills—is the least important. Many of the best journalists learned on the job, with patient editors and forgiving readers. Still, training can be critical. It is then that students of the craft often discover that there is something unique about the field, that it is a calling and not merely a trade. A journalist, deep down, knows that he or she does not work for *The New York Times* or *Emporia Gazette*, though they issue the checks and provide the necessary forum. A journalist works for the public. And ultimately answers to the public alone.

WHY SHOULD JOURNALISTS take an interest in such an abstract issue as "who is a journalist?" Why not simply let the future take its course and welcome the world into our ranks? Because if we do not distinguish ourselves from all others who use this new access, then we and the public we serve shall be the first to lose.

The past is replete with examples of errors and abuses from within our own ranks from the fraudulent Janet Cooke to the most recent CNN debacle known as "Tailwind." We reel from fabrications like those of Stephen Glass, late of *The New Republic*, and former *Boston Globe* columnists Patricia Smith and Mike Barnicle: their errors or missteps were used to defame all journalists. The half-lives of such breaches of professionalism go on for what feels like an eternity, confirming the worst suspicions of those who never did trust the press.

There is no effective way to contain errors and public loss of confidence. Already working journalists are lost in the blur called "The Media," lumped together with disparate industries with whom they have little in common. In a world that does not discriminate between the blunders and excesses of one branch of media and another, it becomes all the more incumbent upon journalists to define themselves— not by pieties and high rhetoric, but by the quality of the work they do day in and day out. That is the only fence they can build to protect themselves from the countless others who perceive themselves as journalists but who show little regard for or understanding of its most basic tenets. The Matt Drudges of this new realm, who claim journalistic victories under a banner of "Often Right," are downright dangerous. Behind Drudge are hordes of others who by default or whim will stumble into the field, wreaking havoc. These newcomers may arrive without any past or way to judge their credibility, and they may disappear just as quickly, as evanescent as a retired URL.

The ancient Romans spoke of a *cursus honorum*, a ladder or path of honor, which one ascended by rungs, earning one's place over time by careful preparation, training and dedication. Those for whom journalism is a career have a vested interest in setting themselves apart from those for whom it is mere sport. At risk is more than just the standing of professional journalists. Unable to discriminate between the credible and the misleading, the public could tune us all out, damaging public discourse and producing not an informed citizenry but an audience of cynics. In the end, what sets the professional journalist apart from the chorus of voices heard all around us is that we put a premium on credibility, recognize it as our sole asset, our only stock and trade. If we were to allow it to be sullied, we would be left with nothing— just another indistinguishable voice on the page, on the screen or in cyberspace.

Who then is a journalist? Anyone who recognizes and protects the sanctity of what we do, who subscribes unswervingly to an ethical canon grounded in balance, fairness, restraint and service. Published on-line or in print, it matters not.

While democracies are best when debate is raucous and utterly uninhibited, journalists can and should let their voices be heard in defense of those traditional values that they hold dear and set them apart from the "casualness and opportunism" that Mencken observed threatens to erode credibility.

Balance, fairness, restraint and service: the most promising future for journalism is rooted in its time-honored values. That should be seen not as a bar, but as an invitation to anyone who understands and will uphold the unwritten covenant between journalists and the public they serve.

Ted Gup teaches journalism at Georgetown University. He has written for The Washington Post, Time *and* National Geographic, *and is currently writing a history of the CIA.*

Who's a Journalist?—II

Welcome the new journalists on the Internet.

Mike Godwin

"I had stumbled upon an important fact: you become a reporter by saying you're a reporter. No qualifications. No license. Almost no training."
—RICHARD REEVES, *What the People Know: Freedom and the Press*

TEN YEARS AGO, it was too expensive for any but a few to play the journalism game in any meaningful way. To reach the kinds and sizes of audience that the traditional news media reached, you had to be rich enough to own your own newspaper or radio or TV station. Or you had to work for someone who did.

But the computer revolution has changed the economics of mass media, including news media. And by lowering the barriers to entry, the Internet has created a whole new class of potential journalists— think of this group as "the cheap journalists." And join me in celebrating their arrival on the scene.

With a $1,000 desktop computer and a connection to the Internet, anybody can reach an audience of thousands or millions—the kind of audience that once only a Hearst or a Murdoch could reach. Nowadays, all you have to be is a Matt Drudge. (You may aim higher than Drudge does, but the beauty of the new medium is that you don't have to be any richer than he was.)

THESE DAYS I sometimes find myself in debates with newsmen about whether the new generation of people publishing on the World Wide

Web qualifies as "journalists." Perhaps not surprisingly, these professionals are often eager to draw some kind of dividing line between what they do for a living and what others are doing—often part-time or for free—on the Internet. The argument takes two forms: either the new on-line writers are "not journalists," or, if they are, they represent a looming disaster for journalism. Here are four of the most common arguments, along with my answers to them.

1. "How can they be journalists if they've got no editors?"

Journalists who've put in their time at newspapers—learning their beats, facing the demands of experienced editors, collecting clips, working their way up—often look with disdain on the would-be Web journalist who's working out of his home office or garage. "How can Mr. On-line Guy learn to be a journalist if he didn't go through what I went through?" they ask. "I needed the city editor to tell me how to write a graceful sentence, and I was a year into the job before I could craft a decent lede?"

The assumption here is that only the distinct process of apprenticeship that most newspaper reporters endured throughout this century can teach you to write well or research well. But there are other traditions of professional training—often traditions that derive from wholly separate professions—that may serve just as well in training the Internet reporter to do his job well. I often say that the best training I ever got as a reporter was when I was a graduate student of English literature—misquote a source there and you flunk, and you're equally doomed if you don't know how to support your assertions with research and evidence.

What's more, it's helpful to have a little faith in the readership and in the power of the marketplace. The Internet is the most feedback-friendly mass medium ever to be invented, and those who publish on-line tend to get direct and immediate assessments of whether they're being elegant or persuasive. It's not always a smooth ride, but writers who listen to their critics tend to get better. And those who don't never would have benefited from an editor in any case. Time after time I've seen on-line writers with no professional training become more effective, more careful writers and reporters. Like stones smoothed by the river current, their styles have become more polished in the wash of public feedback.

2. "It will be harder to tell truth from fiction and rumor. Once it's possible for anyone to write and publish something that has the ap-

pearance of being 'real' journalism, the public is likely to be fooled by frauds and phonies. The prohibitive economics of news-gathering operations has ensured that only the genuine article—the true professional journalist—gets heard. Now that anybody can, in effect, publish his own news reports—perhaps better designed and more graphically pleasing than The Wall Street Journal *or* The New York Times— *won't there be a Gresham's law effect in which all the bad, phony journalism drives out the good, true stuff?"*

The arrogance implicit in this argument is breathtaking, and there are two dimensions to it. The first arrogant premise is that the good, true stuff—the kind of journalism that's essential to the operation of an open society and to an educated citizenry—is the preserve of big media institutions, while the two-bit hackwork is what the garage-band newcomers do. But while we owe a great debt to institutions like *The Washington Post* and *The Wall Street Journal* for the best work they've done, we also need only read A.J. Liebling's *The Press*—with its methodical analyses of the routine distortions that big newspapers regularly inflicted on stories—to get over the fantasy that institutional journalism is *necessarily* any better than a freewheeling collection of net.yahoos. What's more, from Samuel Johnson to I.F. Stone there's a tradition of solo-operator journalists, a tradition older and perhaps more venerable than that of the institutional news media, which strongly suggests that a well-informed individual who applies sober judgment to carefully researched facts can produce reports of enduring value. Journalism as a whole will thrive in the next few decades as more and more individuals with something to say come on-line and start reporting what they see and know.

The second arrogant premise is that the public is an unthinking, unreflective, uncritical consumer of news. Given that the whole idea of freedom of the press is premised on the possibility of an autonomous, thinking citizenry, it's ironic to see how often working journalists put forth this notion of citizen-as-sheep. The reality is that when it comes to news, most citizens have learned to be skeptical, at least to some extent. The people who accept Matt Drudge's political gossip uncritically are the ones who'd believe any scandalous story about Clinton regardless of the source. The rest of Drudge's sizable audience, however, knows to take him with a grain of salt.

3. *"These little guys will never be able to do what the big boys do. No Web-based one-man-show journalist has the resources to do the*

important stories. What made the Washington Post's Watergate sto-
ries effective was not just the abilities of Woodward and Bernstein, but
also the willingness of a major institution like the Post to stand behind
them in the face of withering political attacks."

I do think there's some merit to this argument, but I don't find it completely persuasive. It's certainly useful for us to have large news media institutions that cannot easily be crushed by other political or economic forces. They're heavyweights, but their status comes at a price. Often the commercial compromises that a large publisher has to make (notably those due to dependence on advertising) meant that, in the era prior to widespread Internet publishing, important stories would never see the light of day.

Not long ago, I discussed this question with a professional journalist in an on-line forum. His view was that the important stories required a combination of experience (on the part of a reporter) and resources (on the part of a publisher) that a one-man-operation could never match. "I'd like to see," he wrote, "the average Joe or Jane, say, go spend two months in China and come back with an exhaustive look at human-rights violations." I responded by noting that the average professional newspaper reporter doesn't get that kind of assignment either. Furthermore, I asked him, "do you suppose it's possible that someone who had spent months or years in China might publish something journalistic about human-rights violations without being employed by a newspaper?" The Internet, I insisted, makes that kind of journalistic entrepreneurship possible for someone whose only capital assets are a personal computer and a story to tell.

My friend was skeptical: "Could Everyman have broken the Pentagon Papers story?"

"If Daniel Ellsberg had had access to the Web," I shot back, "would he have needed the *Post* or the *Times*? He could easily have been the first to publish, the *Times* and the *Post* would have followed up the story, and the Pentagon Papers would have been in the news just as much, although perhaps a year earlier."

I think we've seen only the tip of the iceberg when it comes to what's possible for journalism on the Internet. It's not that I think the folks at the big news organizations should be job hunting just yet—they're safe for at least another 30 years, as we still need them for the kind of capital-intensive news gathering and experienced analysis and synthesis that only the pros can offer. But the field is necessarily going to be enriched by the solo players who bring their own special talents to the game. Think about it—our schools have been educating citizens for years to believe that learning about something and writing about what you've learned is a task that every educated person ought to be able to perform. I believe in that principle, and it seems to me that a necessary corollary to it is that every educated person can be a journalist.

4. "What about fairness and accuracy? What happens when there's a sudden influx of amateur journalists who haven't served the kind of ethical apprenticeship that those of us who came up through traditional media organizations have served? Won't those ethical and professional values fall by the wayside?"

This to me is the single hardest issue facing those of us who care about journalism—how do we inculcate ethics among this new, huge wave of practicing journalists, few of whom will have gone to j-school, and few of whom will have been taught by experienced professionals on the job?

I think the answer here is essentially prescriptive—we must actively embrace the new on-line journalists and proclaim them to be journalists. We must offer them support and encouragement, praise and constructive criticism, and, most of all, comradeship. Like St. Peter at the gates of heaven, we must choose to err on the side of letting people in rather than keeping them out. Only by evangelically insisting that the new breed of electronic journalists belong to our religion—and by inviting them to join us and honoring their best work—will we have the kind of influence we want to have on them.

Today, more than ever before, the commercial and political pressures on institutional news media are likely to compromise journalism and foster bad reporting. We should respond to the prospect of independent journalists on the Internet with hope rather than fear or disdain—they represent not just the future but our best hopes for journalism and democracy. Sure, some of them will stumble and make the kinds of mistakes that today's professional news organizations might avoid. But the Net also makes it easier to share our collective wisdom than ever before, and I cheerfully predict that on-line journalists won't keep making the same mistakes over and over again. (Like the rest of us, they'll make helpful new mistakes!)

I'M TRYING NOT to be too much of a sappy utopian here, but if I squint hard enough, I can see a future transformed by an Everyman Journalism that combines the best of traditional news organizations with all the diverse knowledge and insight of a global newsroom on the World Wide Web. If that sounds like science fiction, please understand that my vision is informed in part by contemplation of Gutenberg and the invention of printing with movable type in the 15th century.

Think of how much printing did to shape the modern open society in unanticipated ways. Gutenberg's invention produced cheap books, which put the printed language in the hands of the masses and led directly to the rise of literacy. Once you have a large literate population, the democratic impulse flourishes. Even a moderately educated populace begins to make judgments about its rulers and its mode of government. Cheap book production also advanced both scientific and historical knowledge by ensuring that valuable source documents were preserved, duplicated and shared with many readers. Cheap book duplication quickly made it possible to build a cadre of scientists and historians who had read the same works and shared a common body of knowledge. Finally, movable type made it possible for the past to speak to the future en masse in a way that the evanescent oral tradition never could.

FOR ALL THAT cheap books gave us, I think something equally monumental and equally positive has just been given to us by the Internet, which makes cheap-but-powerful journalism not only possible but inevitable. We face a future in which the First Amendment's Guarantee of freedom of the press becomes co-extensive with its guarantee of freedom of speech. Freedom of the press will become a right for every occupation, not just for the scribbling ones. We can either reject this development or contribute to it our best traditions. And I'm just evangelical enough to think that a marriage of the best of journalism's past and the best of the Internet's future is within our reach.

Mike Godwin, a 1997–98 Media Studies Center fellow, is staff counsel for the Electronic Frontier Foundation. He is author of Cyber Rights: Defending Free Speech in the Digital Age.

What?

Just as Wired *and* Outside *magazines have become print stars by catering to people's individualized interests, TV news itself is becoming a newsstand of options, with the broad, mass-market properties increasingly getting shoved onto the back shelf.*—KYLE POPE

Magazines

A past in paper and a future on the Web

David Abrahamson

PERHAPS EVEN MORE than newspapers, which are geographically limited, and the broadcast media, which are largely derivative—amplifying rather than creating social and cultural trends—magazines reflect and shape their times. In the '50s, the glossy photographs of *Life* and *Look* defined a new era of American abundance. In the '70s, as the political activism of the '60s gave way to the "me decade," city and regional magazines such as *New York* extolled passions for politics and consumer goods. In the '90s, a decade defined by the globalization of commerce and communication, magazines are now in the middle of a new evolution, one distinguished by niche marketing and fertile interaction between print media and the World Wide Web. Where these latest developments will take us is not entirely clear, but it is certain that magazines will both capitalize on and transcend their own recent history.

THE PUBLICATIONS THAT we read today—whether on printed paper or on-line—are decades removed from what might be termed the "golden age" of magazines, the period beginning after World War I and ending in the late 1950s, when several distinct factors brought the American magazine to a then-unprecedented state of development. The first was business strategy. Most magazine publishers, using the commercial model pioneered in the 1890s by Curtis Publishing's *Ladies' Home Journal* and *Saturday Evening Post*, sought large circulations attractive to national advertisers. Most revenue came from advertising sources, while newsstand and subscription prices were kept low, and readers were rarely charged the full cost of producing the publication. As a result, the importance of national advertising grew exponentially.

Also during the same period, a variety of unique types of magazines emerged. In the shifting alignments of American demography and culture, publishers glimpsed new pools of readers and devised new magazine genres to serve them. For example, *Reader's Digest* spoke to America's faith in uplift and self-improvement. *Time* offered busy readers the news in brisk, capsulated form, and before long other newsweeklies were founded on similar formulae. *Time*'s owners also oversaw the creation of three other important titles. In the depths of the Depression, *Fortune* was introduced to shore up the nation's shaken faith in the promise of market capitalism. *Life*, with its pioneering photojournalism, celebrated both the power of the visual image and the marvels of modernity—and was soon imitated by *Look*. With the 1954 founding of *Sports Illustrated*, the heightened role of sports in the national consciousness was accurately foretold.

Other important start-ups of the era include *The New Yorker*, which redefined urbane intellectualism and, in the process, challenged long-standing dominance of *The Atlantic Monthly* and *Harper's Magazine*. *Esquire* offered a new Hemingwayesque urbanity, concerned with style, fashion and other matters of the moment, yet it was also introspective and often certifiably literary. *Playboy* pursued a similar editorial strategy, generously leavened with the mild eroticism of idealized "pictorials." Two other magazines reflected the particular changes reshaping America during the period: the 1945 debut of *Ebony*, founded by John H. Johnson, mirrored the nascent prosperity of the emerging African-American bourgeoisie, while the first appearance of *TV Guide* in 1953 followed the ubiquitous success of the new medium.

A final aspect of their mid-century "golden age" is the extent to which magazines came to serve as indelible markers of the prevailing social reality. The United States emerged from the Depression and World War II poised on the cusp of unparalleled affluence; an unprecedented percentage of the population—more than two-thirds by most measures—would soon claim membership in an expanding middle class. As a reflection of this social and cultural transformation, magazines, particularly the general-interest publications serving mass audiences, enjoyed a special place in American life. By helping both to define and reinforce the communal, consensual and conformist values of American society in the years after World War II, magazines became the dominant medium for the popular discourse of the nation.

SHORTLY BEFORE 1960, however, the magazine industry began to undergo a major transformation, away from serving mass audiences and toward smaller, more specialized readerships. An essential factor in the success of the smaller, more targeted magazines was the changing nature of marketing and advertising during this period. Mass-market advertising revenues, long the lifeblood of the large general-interest magazines, were being siphoned off by television. First introduced in 1947, commercial television's advertising revenues surpassed those of magazines in 1954; less than 10 years later its ad income was double that of magazines. Unable to compete, the three flagship mass-audience magazines, the weeklies *Life*, *Look*, and *The Saturday Evening Post* all ceased publication between 1969 and 1972. Yet at the same time, computerized techniques for finely focusing marketing efforts at specific groups of prospective customers made the more narrowly defined audiences of specialized magazines particularly attractive to advertisers and smaller magazines prospered. Moreover, advances in production and printing technology reduced costs, eliminating many economies of scale and improving the profitability of smaller circulation publications.

In concert with television's ascendancy in the 1960s, the advent of "niche" publishing, with its increasing emphasis on the segmentation of audiences, removed magazines from their central place in popular culture. But by explicitly striving to serve the specific informational needs of particular niches, the magazine industry as a whole prospered. Trade and association magazines, for example, did notably well during this period, and by the 1990s there were more than 10,000 titles published regularly in the United States. Similarly, consumer magazines flourished.

For instance, those devoted to specific personal interests, particularly leisure pursuits, blossomed; *Car and Driver* and *Road & Track*, *Boating* and *Sail*, *Flying* and *Pilot*, *Skiing* and *Ski* were all founded in the late 1950s and early 1960s, and subsequently were turned into notably profitable enterprises by less prominent magazine publishers such as Ziff-Davis, Times Mirror and Hearst.

IN SOME CASES, established magazine genres benefited; both religious periodicals of all denominations and "handyman" magazines for the do-it-yourselfer proliferated. In others, whole new categories of magazines emerged. These included a new breed of city/regional magazine, largely modeled on *New York* founded in 1967, featuring a combination of investigative journalism and shopping advice; a wide variety of self-awareness and self-improvement magazines ranging from *Ms.* to *Psychology Today* to *Self* to *Men's Health*; and magazines such as *PC Magazine* and *PC World*, which earned record revenues from the microcomputer craze of the late 1980s. Other narrowly focused magazines offered everything from conservative cultural politics (*The New Criterion*) to manic humor (*National Lampoon*) to monomaniacal domesticity (*Martha Stewart Living*) to relief for the indigestions (*Cooking Light*) and parental angst (*Family Life*) of middle-aging baby boomers.

Which brings us to the present—and, hence, to the future. It is now clear that the fractionization and proliferation that began in the early 1960s continue to be defining aspects of magazine publishing today. More than 2,000 consumer titles are currently available, and some 900 new titles are launched every year (though the historical record suggests that only a small fraction of these start-ups will actually succeed). Two significant and interrelated consequences arise from the dominantly niche-building nature of the industry, and they will play an important role in determining the future of the magazine form for the next five to 15 years. One is driven by the emerging economic realities of the medium; the other, by the new technological possibilities that magazine publishers, with their expertise at editing for and marketing to specific audiences, are uniquely positioned to take advantage of.

THE U.S. MAGAZINE industry is at present quite healthy and profitable, with more than $13 billion in annual advertising income and $9 billion in circulation revenue, according to the Audit Bureau of Circulations. Moreover, the Magazine Publishers of America, the industry trade group, reports that the total number of magazine readers has increased by 6 percent in the last decade. But, in large measure the result of the dominant fractionization-and-proliferation paradigm, significant business issues, particularly in the realm of circulation, exist—and are likely to influence the future course of the industry.

For example, the costs of building or maintaining circulation are increasing. Magazines with paid circulations rely heavily on the buying of lists of prospective subscribers and mailing offers to them. But the response rates to promotional subscription mailings have been declining for the last few years. In the recent past, a net response rate to a direct-mail circulation promotion of 2 percent was considered acceptable; now 1.5 percent is closer to the norm. As a consequence, publishers have to spend more to maintain their "rate bases"—the levels of circulation promised to advertisers. With newsstands more crowded with more titles, single-copy sales have also become more difficult, and publishers have occasionally gone to great lengths to try to increase them. Consolidation among magazine wholesalers, who control the nation's newsstands and used to number in the hundreds, has left just over 50 in business today. As a result, the wholesalers' bargaining position with magazine publishers has strengthened considerably, and publishers' share of the income from newsstand sales has declined from an average of 45 percent of the cover price to 37 percent. In addition, wholesalers have been able to levy surcharges for special handling or premium placement of newsstand copies.

Moreover, these ongoing stringencies on the circulation side of the magazine business, many the result of the fractionization of the market and a proliferation of titles, are matched by similar issues on the advertising front. The heart of the matter is increasing demands by major advertisers for negotiated (read *discounted*) advertising rates and magazine-funded "value added" merchandising programs.

ALL OF WHICH suggests why the potential represented by the World Wide Web may offer commercially attractive possibilities for the future of the magazine. Tremendous advances in both computer and communications technology have made possible newly efficient ways of distributing greater quantities of needed information. By the late 1990s, it was clear that much of the innovation in these "new media" areas would be led by magazine firms. In the main, the reason for this has been the fortuitous convergence between the strengths (and needs) of the magazine industry and the emerging directions in which the Web seems to be evolving.

These will include at least four significant trends, the first of which is specialization. In many ways, the development of the on-line realm has followed the historical model of magazine development: mass vehicles that, over time, evolve to define and serve specific niches. In the beginning of the on-line world, many of the newly created sites were fairly general in their orientation. Today, however, despite the widely reported soaring stock prices of "portals" such as Yahoo! and Lycos, the dominant on-line trend seems to privilege significant content specialization. As in the conventional magazine world, beyond the gateway afforded by the portal, there will be more different sites serving more different audiences—and, driven by diverging audience interests, the content of the sites themselves is in turn becoming more differentiated.

A corollary of specialization will be that fewer and fewer magazine Web sites will identically mirror the hard-copy print version of the publication. No longer will the Web site be a mere archive of the print product. Many magazine publishers will come to believe that other principles of conception and presentation apply on-line.

However, no industrywide agreement has as yet emerged on the operative principles to be applied when taking information originating in print form and putting it on-line. Some publishers, for example, believe that the average reader's on-line attention span is limited to one screen's worth of information; others think that as many as five screens are acceptable. Some believe that on-screen flashing banner advertising makes no difference; others find it an abomination. With all the different on-line presentation solutions currently in use, it is evident that there is as yet very little unanimity on trade practices.

In contrast, in the traditional print world, both the visual constituent components—headline, deck, body copy, lead paragraph, lead art, callout and caption—and their interrelation are well established, having evolved into their current form over the last 100 years. But the same does not exist on-line yet, in large part because the way information is visually consumed on-line is so different from the way it is consumed on the printed page. Given the limitations of a conventional computer monitor, how the on-line reader actual reads is determined by all manner of visual field factors, cognition/learning theory considerations and ergonomic issues. These are topics about which people have strong opinions, but it is likely that a generally agreed-upon solution, the received wisdom, will soon emerge.

A SECOND MAJOR point of coevolution between the magazine and the World Wide Web will be the continuing process of commercialization of the on-line world. The economic formula for on-line profitability remains elusive, as Slate's abandonment of subscription charges in early 1999 proved. At present, no one has yet defined a workable model to ensure that an on-line publication is profitable. In the on-line world, there are certainly no guarantees—particularly in the sense, for example, that with a traditional print magazine, with a certain number of advertisers willing to pay a certain advertising rate to reach a certain number of readers and with a certain level of operating costs, you can be assured of making money. On-line, such reliable models do not yet exist, but it seems only a matter of time before they will.

Nevertheless, as with most media products, the general principle of keeping costs low and perceived value to the consumer high does seem to pertain on-line. An interesting current example of this, which may serve as a future template for other magazine publishers, is the on-line publication *Salon*, an upscale magazine of politics, culture and literature. Its 1999 advertising rate, expressed in terms of cost per 1,000 (CPM), is from $20 to $40, which is a number from which a set of inferences can be drawn. In comparison, the median CPM for U.S. consumer magazines is approximately $30. At the low end of the scale are undifferentiated media aimed at mass audiences with no great proclivity to consume; television, for example, has an average CPM of about $5-$10 for a 30-second spot. The major newsmagazines with large undifferentiated audiences have CPMs in the $15 to $20 range. Many women's magazines are in the $20 to $25 range. More specialized publications, however, can charge their advertisers between $40 and $60, because their readers both form a well-defined market that advertisers want to reach and are more active consumers.

So the fact that an on-line magazine, *Salon*, can charge an advertising CPM of as high as $40 is significant. In market terms, it validates the notion that, in the view of *Salon*'s advertisers, the right kind of people are regularly reading the publication and, because of who they are and how they spend, these are the readers that advertisers are willing to pay a premium to reach. As a result, by keeping costs low and editorial value high—and therefore attractive to the readers that advertisers desire—*Salon* currently reports a modest profit.

A THIRD FORECAST about magazines' future engagement with the on-line world will focus on a predictable range of commitment on the part of the enterprises that one might presume would be involved. Some media firms have committed and are likely to continue to devote substantial resources in staff and funding to their on-line presence. Time Warner, for example, has spent millions of dollars on its Pathfinder site. Less tangibly but perhaps equally revealing, the third name at the very top of the Time Warner corporate masthead is the person in charge of the firm's on-line efforts. The title is editor of new media, and its prominent position in the corporate hierarchy is perhaps emblematic of the company's commitment to realizing the on-line potential of its publications.

At the other end of the scale will be a small number of prominent publishing firms that one might assume would be heavily involved in the on-line development of their print products—and yet for the next few years they will remain tentative and uncommitted in their approach. In one sense, however, this cautious strategy may have a self-fulfilling dimension to it. The fewer resources devoted to on-line development, the less interesting and useful the resulting site will be. The less compelling the site, the fewer readers it will attract. And the more modest the number of hits the site receives, the more convinced decision-makers will be that the company's on-line investment should be kept to a minimum. In many such cases, it will be clear that senior executives are responding to internal norms of their firm's prevailing corporate culture concerning matters of both risk and technology. As one might expect, between these two poles—the truest of believers at one end and the skeptical at the other—will lie a full spectrum of involvement. By all present indications, this vast range of commitment, viewed as a trend, is likely to persist for the foreseeable future.

A FOURTH AND final point that underscores the promising future of magazines' on-line potential is especially interesting because few if any observers predicted it: the growing number and importance of women on-line, not only as producers but as consumers of Web-based information. There is a persistent cultural assumption that a predisposition to antipathy exists between females and technology. As a matter of both popular imagination and scholarly inquiry, this is a long-held, historically persistent belief with deep cultural roots. So one of the really fascinating data points to be found in the most current usage figures is the suggestion that approximately 45 percent of the people on-line today are women.

It can, however, be argued with some ease that this should not be surprising. When one examines the aggregate data on media use across platforms (books, television, films, periodicals, etc.), the primacy of female consumption is indisputable. And magazines offer a particularly notable case. In numbers of titles, there are roughly one-and-a-half times more women's magazines than there are men's magazines in the United States. Moreover, in terms of readership, women's magazines on average have twice the circulation of men's magazines. What these two comparisons mean in aggregate is that three-quarters of all magazine readers in the country are women. With the growing number of women on-line—which is an expanding subset of the growing number of women who are comfortable using computers—it is likely that the 1999 figure of 45 percent will increase dramatically over the next five years. Stated another way, there is no reason to believe that the current gender proportions of the readership of traditional magazines and the future gender proportions of their on-line versions will, over the long run, show any variation.

IT APPEARS THAT the historic adaptability of the magazine form will serve it exceedingly well in the future. The basic strategic model of "narrow-casting"—serving the specific information needs of specific audiences for whom advertisers will pay a premium—will certainly continue to prevail. In large part due to their skill in applying this niche-driven economic model, successful magazine publishers will remain at the forefront of World Wide Web development, providing on-line information derived from, yet not identical to, that contained in their printed versions. And lastly, despite the importance of the Web, it is clear that both as a self-contained, highly targeted information vehicle and as a core "brand" from which other products will be extended, the magazine in its contemporary printed form will continue to demonstrate its efficacy as a source of information and pleasure for its readers, its utility as a marketing vehicle for its advertisers and its viability as a business enterprise for its publishers well into the 21st century.

David Abrahamson, an associate professor at Northwestern University's Medill School of Journalism, is author of Magazine-Made America: the Cultural Transformation of the Postwar Periodical.

Network and Cable TV

From electronic hearth to TV news on demand

Kyle Pope

IN THE END, it was the twin American passions of sex and football that marked the last gasp of the network news business.

Saturday, December 19, 1998. In Washington, Congress is voting on the impeachment of a president for only the second time in history. In New York, the Buffalo Bills and the New York Jets are locked in a bitter play-off battle for a shot at football's Super Bowl.

And at CBS News, once the most respected news organization in the world, anchorman Dan Rather is watching helplessly as CBS chooses football.

The contrast on the tube was, at times, surreal. As CBS's competitors broadcast the roll call of members of Congress impeaching President Clinton for his dalliance with an intern, the most-watched network on TV was forced to update its viewers between quarters and during time-outs. At one point, CBS even used the ultimate sports-television gimmick—the split screen—showing the action on the field on one side and Rather's grim-faced vote count on the other.

While CBS executives defended their decision the next day—after all, CBS only months earlier had ponied up $4 billion to steal the rights to professional football away from rival NBC—the episode nevertheless carried with it a distinctive end-of-an-era feel.

In case anybody had any doubt about it before, it was clear on that Saturday that the network news business had finally run its course. Viewership of the evening news is at a record low. News operations at

63

the networks are bleeding money, as are the companies themselves. And for the first time in our TV generation, at least two of the Big Three networks have actively talked about farming out a chunk of their news-gathering operations to CNN, once a bitter rival. We are watching—or most likely, not watching—as one of the most powerful news vehicles of our time fades away.

Emerging in its place is a made-to-order TV news landscape spun out of the Internet and digital cable television. News, like much of the rest of pop culture in America, is becoming a niche game. Just as *Wired* and *Outside* magazines have become print stars by catering to people's individualized interests, TV news itself is becoming a newsstand of options, with the broad, mass-market properties increasingly getting shoved onto the back shelf. Why settle for a minute and a half of Wall Street action on "World News Tonight" when you can watch a CNBC reporter counting down the ticks of the Dow Jones Industrial Average, or log onto The Street.com and see your individualized portfolio grow as the market soars past 10,000. Want foreign news? Click over to a new digital channel provided by the BBC. Local news? For a subscription fee, there's a regional channel for you as well.

YOU CAN MOURN if you want the end of our idea of a "broadcast"—a place where the entire country can sit down together and get its information. Truth is, our individual communities have simply become too small, our shared activities too few. The dinner hour is over.

After a half-century of dominance, the big networks themselves are in rapid decline. CBS, NBC and ABC have lost tens of millions of dollars over the past year, forcing them to shed hundreds of employees. NBC—the prime-time ratings champ for most of the past decade—has lost nearly a quarter of its viewers this season alone. Of the four big networks, two of them, CBS and NBC, are seen by Wall Street as being on the sale block.

While some of this is the result of the intense competition from cable, which last year surpassed the networks in viewership for the first time ever, network bungling has sped up the decline: first, they paid too much for programming in a last-ditch effort to bring the viewers back. NBC last year shelled out $13 million an episode for "ER," just as many critics were saying that the drama was losing its zip and viewers were getting bored. Result? "ER's" ratings are down sharply this year, and its biggest weekly draw, the actor George Clooney, has bailed out.

Second, the networks have relied on too shallow a talent pool for their ideas, resulting in shows that are derivative, at best. When "ER" executive producer John Wells proposed yet another show about a hard-luck Irish family last year, NBC—which had already invested so much in his medical drama—could hardly afford to say no. The result was "Trinity," a show panned by the critics and, ultimately, canceled by NBC.

In this climate of failure and fear, news stands out as a luxury the networks simply can't afford. The image boost that a news division once provided to the networks is no longer worth the $400 million a year it takes to keep one of these operations afloat. As a result, CBS has held serious talks with CNN about selling off part of its news-gathering operations, as has ABC. The idea is to let cable cover the breaking news, while leaving the networks to focus on newsmagazines and the morning shows, the only two news genres now that consistently make money.

Dan Rather, meantime, has been agitating inside CBS to can the 6:30 p.m. "Evening News" and shift it to a prime-time slot where more people may watch. But, even Rather concedes that may ultimately be too small a step. "Could a network bow out of the news business entirely?" Rather asked me rhetorically, in a conversation in his office just off the "Evening News" set. "I don't think I could argue with you if you said it was probable."

THE END OF the network news comes precisely a half-century after the genre was born, in a 15-minute NBC program hosted by John Cameron Swayze called "The Camel News Caravan." As part of the sponsorship deal, a Camel cigarette had to be burning on the set, and Swayze himself had to take a puff at some point during the broadcast. CBS jumped in later the same year, with a similar show hosted by Douglas Edwards.

Throughout the 1940s and 1950s, TV news was no big deal. When President Eisenhower briefed the nation on military moves off the coast of China, the networks duly taped the bulletin, then ran it after prime time was over. Richard Nixon's "Checkers" speech of 1952 reached the public only because the Republican National Committee bought airtime to run it.

It was the quiz-show scandal of the late 1950s that changed the game. That controversy prompted the Federal Communications Commission to force the networks to air much more "public service" broadcasting as an absolution for their quiz-show sins. To their credit, the mandate was embraced by network chiefs, who saw news as a prestige product that could polish the image of their companies.

By the mid 1960s, Walter Cronkite was hailed by *Time* magazine as the most trusted man in America, adopted as a father figure at a tumultuous time in America, through the civil-rights battles and the Vietnam War, and the resignation of Nixon after Watergate. The bond forged during the Cronkite era between the network news and the viewers who watched it would come to define the next three decades of television, and wouldn't be broken until CNN arrived as a force in the 1980s.

The all-news cable network is, perhaps more than any other single force, responsible for the undoing of the network news business in America. It is more profitable than the three network news divisions combined and, arguably, the most influential. And, it has done all of this despite the fact that hardly anybody watches: on an average day, fewer than 1 percent of Americans tune in to CNN.

But it is the ubiquity of CNN and its half-dozen copycats that have killed the network news business. With more than 75 percent of the country now plugged into cable, it's difficult to argue that America is missing a big news event if it's not on ABC, CBS or NBC. Indeed, Leslie Moonves, the one-time actor who runs CBS Television in Hollywood, cites this fact in defending his decision to show football on the network rather than Congress' impeachment vote. If you want a constant rehashing on the vote, he says, tune in to CNN.

Similar explanations were given by other network news chiefs last year, in defending their decisions not to go live with the resignation of former House Speaker Newt Gingrich, for instance, or with the results of the mid-term Senate elections. The danger, of course, is that viewers begin to assume that the networks won't be there when news breaks, which is precisely what has happened. On the day that CBS made its football decision, CNN received its highest rating of the year. And at several points during the day, more people were watching the cable network than either ABC or NBC, which stuck to the political coverage.

YET IN LOOKING ahead at the future of TV journalism, it's not enough to simply say that the big networks will continue to decline and that cable will continue to grow. Not only is that old news, but it's somehow predictable, given that the three network news divisions now compete against a dozen cable channels offering essentially the same information. A fracturing of the news market is inevitable.

Beyond the decline of broadcast network news as we have known it, a much more revolutionary change is unfolding. For today's big broadcast and cable networks, the arrival of digital TV represents a brutal leveling of the playing field. Distribution is no longer key. Over the next decade, what once was a shortage of space on cable systems and in the airwaves will become a glut, thanks to the shrunken data size of digital video. Being one of the few players rich or established enough to send out a signal will no longer be enough; indeed, being a behemoth will quickly become a disadvantage, as the TV news business transforms itself from a passive medium, where viewers are told what's important, to a participatory one, where they decide for themselves.

For the future of news, instead of evening dinner around the kitchen table think of Sunday lunch at a suburban cafeteria: you will be able to watch—and pay for—only what you're interested in; if you're bored with foreign news, for instance, you needn't be bothered. Already, cable's Fox News is testing the notion of regional sports and news networks, meaning that newscast viewers in the Bronx will soon be able to see a different program than the one beamed to Manhattan's Upper West Side. Imagine the prickly social and racial questions involved in picking different stories for different neighborhoods. It is a quandary that has already been faced by Kraft Foods, which last year began testing a plan to use cable TV to target its commercials at different neighborhoods. Ads for fat-free salad dressing, for instance, might be beamed to an upscale, suburban neighborhood, while an urban neighborhood nearby would get ads for Cheez Whiz and Kool-Aid. If companies aren't careful, say Madison Avenue experts, they could find themselves catering more to stereotypes than to actual consumer tastes.

CNN is working on a plan for news-on-demand, meaning viewers will be able to call up essentially any story, by topic, regardless of what time they tune in. Producers, once the gatekeepers of news and information, are on their way to becoming movie-house ticket-takers, passing on news and entertainment that viewers say they're interested in paying for.

Driving all of this is the shift to digital television, already under way in most big cities in America. Because digital data is so much more compact than the analog streams that now go into your television, broadcasters and cable networks soon will be able to quadruple the amount of information they can send out, without buying more channel space. While Congress intended that TV networks use this extra space to offer super-clear high-definition television, few networks are headed in that direction. Instead, they plan to vastly expand the number of choices on offer, even if it's simply several versions of the same signal.

The possibilities in entertainment are endless. ABC, for instance, has been testing the idea of using one of its new channels to replay its soap operas at night, for viewers who work during the day. MTV plans to offer several different versions of its flagship service, each catering to a different genre of music. And PBS, which sees the arrival of digital television as a long-awaited opportunity to reinvent itself, hopes to use the new technology to vastly beef up its educational programming. Brace yourself for Barney in Spanish.

In news, the arrival of digital TV offers a way around the networks' primary conundrum: The fact that fewer and fewer Americans are home at 6:30 to see the evening news. All three networks are toying with the idea of replaying their newscasts later in the evening on a digital channel, and perhaps teaming up with a cable news provider to fill the time the rest of the day.

BUT EVEN THE coming explosion in choices offered by digital TV doesn't capture what's about to happen to TV news. The real revolution, less than a decade away, is in merging those digital TV bits with the World Wide Web. It is that move, thanks to improvements in Internet video, that will ultimately decide the fate of the network news divisions.

Recent moves by NBC and CBS show how seriously executives at the network view the transition. NBC in recent months has made no fewer than 15 major investments in Internet content companies, many of them related to news. It has taken financial stakes in the Snap Internet portal service and in the iVillage news and information site for women. And it has revamped the Web site for CNBC, more closely melding the information provided on the Internet with what appears on the screen. CBS, meantime, has hooked up with Internet giant America Online. Under that deal, CBS News provides content to AOL and mentions the service at the end of Rather's "Evening News." In exchange, CBS gets much-needed cash and a chance to align with the younger, hipper users of AOL.

The flurry of deal-making reflects where news is moving. For the next few years, the action will be in combining what you see on television with data pumped down digital cable lines. Though only a handful of people in the country see it now, NBC already is offering enhanced data along with many of its newscasts. Watch a story on Kosovo and pull up a short history of the crisis. The latest settlement in the tobacco legal wars? Available, on demand, via your television screen.

Soon, though, the entire game will migrate to the Web. Using remote control devices linked to set-top boxes already in production, viewers will be able to call up the programs they want when they want them. Ultimately, once the melding of the TV and the PC is complete, you will be able to "bookmark" news like many people now electronically dog-ear the Internet sites they most watch: stories about the weather, plane crashes and Belgium will be all you have to see, if that's your fancy.

Lost, of course, is the wonderful serendipity of stumbling across news you didn't know you needed, or cared about. And, shifting some of the editorial process to the viewers will only add to our information stress: now, it will be our job to decide what's important, to prioritize the news. In a sense, we are all about to climb inside our television sets, changing the future of news forever.

Kyle Pope is a media reporter for The Wall Street Journal.

Newspapers

*Figure out how to give readers a choice and take your eye
off the quarterly earnings report.*

Leo Bogart

How DOES THE technology-driven communications revolution that is
transforming the world threaten the survival of the established media?
Newspapers are best considered from the perspective of their social
function as sources of public enlightenment and amusement and as
creators of public opinion. They provide their hometowns with a sense
of common identity in a way that other media cannot match. They
command news-gathering resources that even the most prosperous local television news operations cannot remotely match. If they were to
founder, there would be dire effects on social cohesion and on the
integrity of government. But what newspapers can accomplish depends on their health as money-making business enterprises.

Newspapers have survived the arrival of radio and television, but
these are both essentially devoted to entertainment, with news as an
incidental element. The Internet, by contrast, deals in information and
offers unlimited amounts of it in an unending fresh supply. Are newspapers bound to succumb to its fearsome competition? There is no
evidence that time spent on the Web is coming out of the diminishing
amount of time spent in newspaper reading, but the long-term consequences are still uncertain.

EVEN IF THE Internet had not arrived on the scene, newspapers would
still be undergoing profound changes over the next quarter-century—

some forced by the environment and some imposed by their own efforts to remain responsive to readers and advertisers. The trends that will affect the metropolitan daily press are already well established.

Frequency of readership is declining despite the steady rise in household income and in educational attainment. Although nearly nine out of 10 people look at a newspaper over the course of a week, a diminished number of them subscribe and read as a daily habit. (Forty years ago, 80 percent of adults read a paper on a typical day; today only 57 percent do.) The entry of women into the workforce has heightened time pressures in daily life, on men as well as on women. The attrition of the nuclear family has altered the predictable patterns of daily routine in which newspaper reading had a regular place.

Succeeding generations read with ever less frequency. Children are no longer reared with newspapers as a predictable presence in the home, and the attachment to a paper is no longer what it was. The downward trend has been driven in part by the change in the ethnic composition of the population, with a much higher proportion of lower-income nonwhites at the younger ages.

The metropolitan papers that account for the lion's share of all circulation have been especially hit as the balance of the population has shifted from central cities to suburbs. Suburbanites don't identify with the towns where newspapers are published and whose personalities and politics are their traditional news topics.

The number of cities with more than a single daily is steadily shrinking. Papers keep disappearing even in cases where they have combined business operations with their rivals under the Newspaper Preservation Act (which exempts them from the anti-trust laws). Although most small-town dailies still publish in the afternoon, only a handful of big cities still support an evening paper.

Ownership is progressively more concentrated, with fewer surviving family-owned independent newspapers, and a small number of large chains accounting for a growing part of total circulation. Just in the past three years, 420 of the nation's 1500 dailies have been sold. Both to attract regional advertising and to save money through centralized production, acquisitions have often taken the form of clusters at the fringes of metropolitan areas. In some cases, dailies have bought or started suburban weeklies or free-distribution "shoppers" in order to pre-empt new local competition. Curiously, newspapers have not been a major target for the expansionary ambitions of the large multimedia empires. (Disney quickly sold the group of dailies it acquired with its takeover of Capital Cities/ABC.)

Newspapers are losing their share of advertising, both because of the attractions of other media and because of changes in the structure and practices of the retail business, newspapers' mainstay and partner for more than a century. With the introduction of computerized databased marketing systems, retailers have been concentrating more of their promotional efforts against what they call their "core customers," using targeted direct mailings rather than newspaper ads reaching the general public. Non-store retailing in the form of catalog sales, direct-response cable television shopping channels and merchandise offerings on the Internet continue to erode the market position of traditional merchants whose business has relied on newspaper advertising.

Under the pressure of these external forces, newspapers have faced challenges and pursued actions that are likely to continue into the future:

They have adopted new production technology that makes strong use of computerized information management and produces greater efficiency and cost savings. Composition and page makeup are now handled electronically, eliminating large categories of long-established printing crafts and allowing more time for late-breaking news. (Intermediate mechanical stages between the computer and printing plates will soon be eliminated.) High-speed presses offer enhanced color reproduction. Rapid inserting and bundling equipment gives advertisers the capacity to target messages to residents of small geographic areas. Satellite transmission allows some metropolitan dailies to print simultaneously in several different locations of their far-flung markets. It has facilitated the flow of national advertising and has made possible the growth of *USA Today* and *The Wall Street Journal* and of the national edition of *The New York Times*. (Without those national newspapers, newspaper readership would have fallen even more than it has.)

ALTHOUGH NEWSPAPERS HAVE, on the whole, been highly profitable enterprises, their margins have been much lower than those of broadcast media and cable television. Readers have responded poorly to price increases, so daily newspapers' circulation revenues have been held in check. Their advertising has been nibbled by weekly papers distributed free, targeted to limited geographic communities or, with a focus on irreverence and entertainment, to young people who disdain the mainstream press. Newspapers have maintained profitability by cutting production costs and by outsourcing functions (like the composition of display ads) that were formerly done in-house. But there are not too many opportunities for further efficiencies.

Advertising inserts preprinted in excellent color on glossy stock have supplanted run-of-press display advertisements, and a growing proportion of them are distributed selectively to the areas that advertisers want to reach rather than to the newspaper's entire circulation. A parallel and related development has been the creation of zoned editorial sections and the growth of Total Market Coverage plans, which deliver advertising inserts to nonsubscribing households, either by mail or through the newspaper's own carrier force.

This last trend, which has allowed newspapers to compete with direct-mail houses and with other providers of direct delivery, has been made possible by the transformation of newspapers' own distribution methods. Only a few years ago, juvenile carriers accounted for almost all home subscription sales and deliveries. They have been replaced on most metropolitan papers by adults handling large motorized routes, while sales and collections are managed by newspapers directly.

Newspapers have faced diminished retail advertising business as department stores have merged or vanished. Huge discount and other mass merchandisers have come to dominate retailing, and vertically integrated specialty store chains have expanded their market share. The new kinds of stores typically rely on the appeal of their names and locations to initiate traffic rather than on advertisements for specific items. They spend a much smaller percentage of their revenues on ads, a smaller percentage of their advertising budgets in newspapers and all but an infinitesimally small part of their newspaper advertising in inserts. All this makes the main body of the typical daily thinner than it used to be, perhaps diminishing its perceived value for the reader. To replace their lost department store advertising, newspapers have cultivated new categories of advertisers, like computer stores and wireless phone companies. They have become more dependent on classified ads, which have a growing vulnerability to competition from the Internet.

The threat of losing their hold on the classified market drove most newspapers to establish Web sites of their own, in which classified advertising is an important component but which also offer updated news, other current editorial matter and, in some cases, access to archival information. Although most of these sites have thus far been losing money, they are, quite sensibly, regarded as necessary investments to ensure future growth and to pre-empt competitive inroads. The Internet allows users to pick just the information they want, whether it comes from a newspaper Web site or from some other source. This customized flow contrasts with the newspaper's ability to put the same facts and ideas in front of everyone, on subjects readers didn't know they were interested in until they saw them.

While weekday reading has fallen into an erratic pattern, the Sunday edition has maintained greater stability. Since Sunday is the preferred day for advertising inserts, it accounts for a growing proportion of newspaper revenues. With its generous assortment of specialized sections directed at particular kinds of reader interests, a larger part of the Sunday paper is devoted to pastime content, in direct competition with magazines. Newspapers' own locally edited magazine sections, unable to sustain themselves with local advertising, have given way to the two nationally syndicated magazines, *Parade* and *USA Weekend*. Newspapers have also borrowed one of magazines' less attractive habits, producing "advertorial" sections, in which pseudoeditorial matter, written either by an outside agency or by a unit of the advertising department, is interspersed with advertising.

Not only on Sunday but also on weekdays, a growing number of special interest sections and pages (for example, on computers, travel, automobiles, personal finance and home decoration) have been created to lure advertisers as much as readers.

THUS FEATURES OCCUPY a larger percentage of total editorial space, with the hard news of the day taking correspondingly less. This trend is undoubtedly fed by the realization on the part of editors that many readers are already familiar with the headlines they see in the paper. With updated news—general, financial and sports—almost continually available over a number of cable channels and on the Internet, editors are inclined to cede their traditional task of reporting current events to a world that will be amazed to learn them. Although the great advantage newspapers have over electronic news is that they permit sustained narrative and serious analysis, editors increasingly accept the mistaken notion that readers are too impatient to read a long story, especially one that jumps inside from the front page.

This trend has especially affected the coverage of world, national and even statewide news. Only a handful of dailies maintain correspondents abroad, and the pickup of wire-service stories has fallen, especially since the United Press International encountered nearly fatal financial difficulties. Fewer papers are willing to sustain the cost of $250,000 to maintain a one-person foreign news bureau. Aside from *The Wall Street Journal*, which had 100 correspondents collecting economic and financial news, there were only 286 American overseas newspaper reporters in 1998, according to a study by The Project on the State of the American Newspaper. Three newspapers (*The New York Times*, *The Washington Post* and *Los Angeles Times*) maintained 20 or more foreign bureaus. Six other papers and two newspaper groups (Knight-Ridder and Cox) had three or more foreign bureaus. Much closer to home, coverage of news from the 50 state capitals is left to the wire services by most of the nation's 1500 dailies. Only 113 wire-service reporters and 513 reporters for individual papers were covering statehouses, even though the actions of state governments have intimate repercussions on every locality.

"Local, local, local" has become an editorial shibboleth, though it is not easy to define what is local in a sprawling metropolitan region. It may well be that what attracts readers to local stories is not so much that they offer connections to familiar locales and personalities as that they are written fresh and have not been seen anywhere else first.

Who is to judge what's news and what isn't? Publicly held newspaper corporations are run increasingly by professional managers rather than by individuals steeped in the tradition of public service journalism. With management attention focused on the bottom-line requirements for survival, newspapers have become increasingly enamored of the marketing precept that product design should be fitted to customers' desires (in the spirit of the old department store adage, "Give them what they want"). Editors have always tried to please their readers, but in an earlier era they did so by letting their own instincts lead them to create compelling and innovative content. In recent years, editors have been encouraged to become more attuned to their own managerial responsibilities to the enterprise, to work more closely with the advertising and circulation departments in developing new subjects to cover and to rely more heavily on research as a guide to what they should and should not print.

As newspapers become monopolies in their own communities, they tend to become bland and fearful of giving offense to any segments of their constituencies. Where competing papers often had sharply expressed and polarized viewpoints, survivors typically try to publish a range of opinions on their editorial and op-ed pages, much as they expand their comics pages to include the most popular strips of their defunct competitors. Some newspapers have abandoned the practice of endorsing candidates in electoral campaigns. Others have dropped daily editorials. They are less certain of their role as leaders of public opinion.

Newspapers have been conservatively run, averse to risk and unwilling to make the kind of investment in research and development that characterizes growth industries. As part of their heightened emphasis on cutting costs, many have skimped on personnel, reducing their news staffs and allowing salaries to drift below levels set by other organizations. Each year, a smaller number of journalism school graduates, and not always the most talented, choose newspaper careers.

MOST OF THE TRENDS that I have just outlined have occurred slowly. Projected ahead by a quarter-century, they seem unlikely to produce a radical transformation in newspapers' functions or position as a major medium of information, recreation and advertising. This doesn't mean that upheavals are out of the question. Small changes in revenues can translate into large changes in profitability. The health of individual newspapers can be severely affected by minor events like the demise of a local department store or a sharp hike in the cost of newsprint.

In the final analysis, the future of newspapers depends on their ability to sustain their mass readership base. Newspapers with large circulations have lost advertising and failed because their numbers were slipping. Newspapers will continue to be dependent on advertising as their principal revenue source. It is unlikely that they will shift to free distribution in the next 25 years, even though it might be economically advantageous for them to do so. Advertisers have continued to consider paid circulation as an indicator of reader regard and attentiveness, even though newspapers have succumbed to the self-defeating practice of according readership figures, based on surveys, greater weight than the count of actual copies sold.

Although many of the trends I have outlined seem adverse, they must be seen in the context of the broader changes taking place in the communications business. The size of the television audience has been relatively constant (though it would be affected by the emergence of video entertainment on the Web), but that audience has been progressively fractionated by the multiplication of channels. There can be no reversal of the sharp decline in the TV networks' ratings. Television's cost efficiency for advertisers must inevitably plunge, leaving newspapers in a stronger competitive position (although far short of an advantage, given the way that cost-per-1,000 is conventionally calculated). Television delivers ever narrower segments of the public and accumulates audience reach by repeating commercials on different stations and at different times. By contrast, newspapers provide advertisers with simultaneous access to a wide spectrum of readers in every locality.

There will be no reversal of the trend toward greater concentration, but this will come about more through additional mergers of existing chains rather than through purchase of the few hundred remaining independent papers, most of them small. On the whole, small papers in isolated communities have shown fewer circulation losses than average, but small papers are especially vulnerable to the attrition of advertising caused by the relentless march of the Wal-Marts. Some of these papers will have to switch from daily to less frequent publication schedules, but most of them will keep on going. The three high-quality papers with the most cosmopolitan perspective (*The New York Times*, *The Washington Post* and *Los Angeles Times*) have retained their circulation far better than other large metropolitan papers. Most dailies will be facing some difficult editorial choices if their audiences continue to wane. Should they cling to their past mission of addressing the concerns of the whole mass public in the areas they cover, or should they acknowledge that they have become providers to an information-hungry elite? If they were to accept this latter role, they would have to let their editors' news judgments prevail over the chatter of focus groups. They would devote more attention to serious news of the wider world and less to trivia. Undoubtedly, their circulation numbers would gradually drop, and some categories of advertising would wither. With modifications of their rate structures, they might, however, end up with greater revenues than they enjoy now.

The chief imponderable, of course, pertains to the growth of the

Internet and the degree to which it will siphon off readers and ads. No one can predict this with any certainty, nor guess the eventual effect of wireless handheld personal digital assistants equipped with screens that can display information. One crucial reason why newspapers have ploughed on through the age of broadcasting is that print, with its use of symbols to express thought, represents a different form of communicating facts and ideas than broadcasting messages at the pace of the human voice. Television offers no equivalent for the eye's ability to ferret out pertinent information from the recesses of the complex, densely packed newspaper page. Neither does the computer screen. Some cable all-news channels now carry a number of different flows of information: a talking head, news headlines, financial data, sports results, the weather—all going simultaneously and competing for attention. A newspaper page has a similar multiplicity of offerings, but they are static; the reader is in control and can jump from one item to another as interest or curiosity impels. This unique characteristic, along with the advantages of tactility, will continue to differentiate newspaper reading from reading the computer (or the modem-adapted television) screen, even as new software makes data more rapidly and easily accessible than it is at present, and as the screen itself is reduced to the bulk of a paper tablet.

IF THE FUTURE of newspapers is uncertain, that does not mean that it is beyond influence or control. Is there a recipe for continued success? Maybe, with the right ingredients. Here is my advice to the industry's leaders:

1. Make circulation growth the highest priority, with constant tests of pricing, promotional and sales techniques, and new distribution methods. Put the appropriate pressure behind Newspaper-in-Education programs that introduce the reading habit to youngsters who will never pick it up at home.

2. Keep the wall between Church and State. Of course editors and reporters should understand that they have a stake in the business success of the enterprise, but that is not the same as giving marketers control of the newsroom or of the editorial product. Research should be used to stimulate thinking, not to provide direction. And the research should be valid, please. Focus groups should be used the way they were meant to be used, to introduce subjects for proper study, not to substitute for solid evidence.

3. Go after the opportunities in national advertising. With the demise of most of the old newspaper representative firms that handled competing dailies, there are today only a handful of salespeople making calls to sell the medium. Media are selected, using questionable formulas, by advertising agencies and media buying services staffed with young people who often rarely look at a paper themselves. They must be painstakingly educated. That requires sales talent and a constant infusion of fresh, provocative research about how advertising works. And all this takes money.

4. Consider your Web site a distinctive product rather than a mere spin-off from what you print. The Internet can offer profitable opportunities to exploit the full range of copy and data that you generate, receive or keep in storage. It allows specific items of news and advertising to move selectively to the people who want it. But it is not a substitute for the comprehensive, easily accessible newspapers you publish now. Don't let it divert your attention.

5. Figure out how to give readers a choice. The end of competition among local dailies has a lot to do with the loss of readers. Advertisers don't like duplicated readership, but not all of them have the same objectives. In some parts of the world, newspapers have carved out new markets for youth-oriented daily tabloids that emphasize sports and entertainment. Figure the marginal incremental costs on top of your existing production and overhead and see whether this isn't worth a try.

6. Take your eye off the quarterly earnings report. Spend what's required to stay competitive in R&D and to cultivate talent at every level of the organization. That's easier to say than to do, but in the long run there's no alternative to doing it.

Leo Bogart, a 1989–90 Media Studies Center fellow, is the former executive vice president and general manager of the Newspaper Advertising Bureau. He is author of Preserving the Press: How Daily Newspapers Mobilized to Keep Their Readers *and* Commercial Culture: The Media System and the Public Interest.

When?

In our thirst for speed we must not lose sight of credibility and context. Being first doesn't matter one whit if you are wrong.—DAVE KANSAS

What's the Rush?

An e-epistolary debate on the 24-hour news clock

Dave Kansas and Todd Gitlin

tgl@is.nyu.edu

DEAR TODD:

In financial news, time is money. And with the advent of the Internet, the ability to deliver financial news throughout a 24-hour cycle has presented mainstream news organizations with both opportunities and challenges.

The concept of 24-hour news gets a lot of journalistic thinkers in a tizzy. The speed of it all leads to mistakes that could be avoided in a more traditional newspaper cycle. Moreover, the dynamic pace can sometimes lead to a loss of context. To the traditionalist, the 24-hour cycle has become a nightmare of drivel and error.

But this nervous carping about the 24-hour news cycle belies an important fact: the concept of 24-hour financial and business news is not a new thing. The financial wire services, Dow Jones, Reuters and Bloomberg chief among them, have been providing professionals with real-time news for many years. But the Internet has brought that news to a wider population.

On Wall Street, information is the currency of the realm. Before the Internet, only professionals had access to this 24-hour news cycle. Now all investors can gain access. This democratization of information is not harmful, but rather it is empowering.

The Internet is at the heart of the 24-hour news revolution. And it presents a very tough challenge—it is one thing to cheer the democratization of information, it is another thing to execute on this new playing field. Working on the Internet requires a bold combination of accuracy, quality and timeliness. The Internet journalist must combine the lessons of television (timeliness) with the lessons of print (depth, accuracy and context) in order to produce the sharpest products in this new medium.

The 24-hour news cycle and the Internet are not going to go away. Indeed, news is going to become more ubiquitous in coming months and years, especially in the financial space. The lengthening trading day, the global nature of financial transactions and the increasing pool of individual investors guarantee a healthy appetite for more 24-hour news. The winners will incorporate the important lessons of quality taught by traditional print media into this new world.
—Dave

dkansas@thestreet.com
DEAR DAVE:

To the fraternity of nervous carpers, the 24-hour news cycle is a tempting target indeed. In the area of business news, opening up instant informational access to legions of on-line traders looks nifty as long as the market is soaring; it won't look so nifty during downturns. And it certainly hasn't done much for the Asian and Latin American economies that have, in recent months, watched billions of dollars gurgle down the drain in milliseconds flat.

In the larger realm of news, one need only speak the magic word "Lewinsky" to indicate one danger. Reporting of the Clinton sex scandal gave haste a bad name. In a world of news Web sites, the risks of error are obvious—even more obvious than the risk of error stemming from leaky prosecutors. Rushing to get scraps of "news" on-line before somebody else did during the early months of scandal coverage, *The Dallas Morning News* and *The Wall Street Journal* did themselves no honor by relaying rumors they couldn't substantiate. The all-chat, much-guesswork, even-more-opinion-and-attitude TV news channels had all those hours to burn and a shortage of reporting or useful analysis. Where would Chris Matthews' "Hardball" be without insinuation? Shorter, for one thing.

But as you rightly say, the speed-up did not arrive yesterday. The 24-hour cycle accelerates a rush that was already maniacal. The loss of context that you mention is not a loss of something we had in abundance the day before yesterday. Rather, News Lite has become News Liter. What we face, and what I deplore, is not an acceleration from zero to 60, but the move from 60 to 80—hazardous, yes, error-prone, yes, but not a loss of some impeccable news standard of steadiness and thoroughness that we not so long ago held dear.

Even Matt Drudge's role in the speed-up has been blown way out of proportion. Poor Mr. Drudge has claimed piles of credit, and been saddled with piles of blame, for leaking the initial Starr-Lewinsky-Tripp story that *Newsweek* was sitting on, way back in January 1998. Very good public relations for Mr. Drudge, but the far bigger deal is that *Newsweek* held its own story for a week at the behest of Kenneth Starr. *Newsweek* might have good reasons for stopping the clock, but it should not have been colluding with the prosecutor. Even we carpers can't blame the speed-up for the morass of unsourced or semi-sourced journalism that swallowed American journalism for many months.

We live in a speed culture, a culture that invites people, including investors, including journalists, to become speed freaks—to jump the gun, move it, get there fastest with the mostest. We love the rush—more when we win than when we lose, to be sure. No doubt lemmings love the rush too—during the gallop en masse toward the precipice, and perhaps never so much as during that delicious moment when they take leave of the soil and feel the air surging into their faces.
—Todd

DEAR TODD:

Speed thrills and speed kills, as you rightly point out.

I am gratified that you wisely take your concerns about the pace of 24-hour news and address more than just the Internet. The proliferation of 24-hour cable television news, old-line newspapers working on-line and pure Internet news outlets all find themselves running afoul of time-honored standards. It is not just an Internet problem—the 24-hour beast is creating challenges for all news organizations.

But some of your worries don't make much sense. I find it particularly troubling when you say that opening up instant access to information to legions of on-line traders is "nifty" when the market is soaring, but terrible if the market turns south. Is information about finance and investing something that the populace should be protected from as though it were pornography? Wall Street's big institutions would have us believe that only their good, honest brokers should be privy to this kind of information, and apparently you share that view. As a journalist, I believe that individuals have a right to information about their investments and the world of finance. Indeed, I think providing financial news and information to the masses goes to the core of what journalism is all about. Will some people abuse this information and find themselves in some sort of trouble? No doubt. The same thing happens with sports news and gamblers. That's no reason to argue that sports news should be limited in some manner to protect gamblers from themselves.

Still, your concerns about speed and "news lite" and "liter" are well founded, and I share those concerns. I am embarrassed by what passes for local television news and can't bear to watch the nattering on cable television. As the editor of an on-line publication, I have preached hard to my staff about the need for rigorous reporting and adherence to the highest standards. Good will comes slowly and painfully, and it is easy to destroy it—in any medium. In our thirst for speed we must not lose sight of credibility and context. Being first doesn't matter one whit if you are wrong. This is especially true in financial news, where credibility is vital and where those who trash their credibility by being first and wrong will not survive long. In many respects financial news is a self-correcting marketplace where inaccuracy is rewarded with failure.

What I hear from you, and others, is simple fear of the 24-hour news cycle. Speed is thrilling, you say, and those who get hooked on the speed of 24-hour news lose sight of accuracy and become like lemmings racing headlong toward the cliff's edge. But all of that fear is not going to make the growth of continuous and ubiquitous news go away. It is unfortunate that in the current environment, many of the best journalists and editors, fearful of 24-hour news, turn their nose up at the Internet, mocking its integrity and clinging close to the dead-tree world of newspapers and magazines. There is indeed a great battle for journalistic standards taking place on the Internet, but the fact is that the best and brightest are not sufficiently engaged. If more strong journalists and editors could get past their fear and dive into this new world, those of us fighting for credibility would stand a better chance of shaping this medium so that it reflects the standards and credibility that we all crave.

—Dave

DEAR DAVE:

Somehow I seem to have become a tool of traditional brokers, simply by expressing doubt about the glories of warp speed. Whew! That's the sort of leap that gives Luddites a warm righteous feeling, for if our only choice is between rapturous embrace of every new technology, just because it's fast, and automatic rejection, also just because it's fast, we are left with faith in the fast—which is too much faith for me. Is it not possible to express some apprehension about the social good of the speed-up without being tarred with a reputation for horse-and-buggy censoriousness or a surrender to giant corporations? Is it not possible to find something, well, *funny* about the wild hunger for easy money?

Let me take the opportunity to answer my own questions: Skepticism makes sense. Censorship is not the sole alternative to unbridled enthusiasm. Doubt is a fine alternative.

You now argue that whenever markets succeed in arousing public interest, that's dandy for society—which would be a consistent position if it also favored public trading in heroin, sarin gas or women. If, on the other hand, we do not assume that whatever is, is good, we admit that, in principle, some restraint might make sense. It would follow, further, that if voluntary restraint fails, society may have an interest in involuntary restraint. While I have no particular interest in regulating on-line trading, I do not see easy-access trading as an unblemished good any more than unbridled gambling is. The danger that still needs addressing is that fast-moving information fuels delusions about getting rich quick. Let's post some signs: DANGER: GOLD RUSH AHEAD—NOT EVERY DIG PANS OUT.

We may not want to regulate the smooth flow of sports stats, but don't the dependents who stand a chance of becoming impoverished have a stake in limiting the gambling use that is made of sports stats? As for the self-correcting market, well, wouldn't it be nice to spare a lot of people the risk of impoverishment before the corrections kick in and they find themselves corrected out onto the street?

Let me summarize what I was trying to say about speed and the news cycle. What I propose is not simple fear but complicated fear. *Laissez-faire* is fine up to a point. The interesting, difficult and necessary question is, up to what point? News organizations are hog-wild over speed, and cool to frozen over making the world more intelligible. This imbalance has to be deplored—not because speed isn't

sometimes useful, or fun, but because speed is a fabulous drug. And drugs are trouble not because they don't work but because they do. We already inhabit a civilization that cherishes speed over deliberation. Call me grumpy, but I can't get enthusiastic about more of the same.
—Todd

Dave Kansas is editor-in-chief of TheStreet.com. *Todd Gitlin, a 1998– 99 Media Studies Center fellow, is professor of culture, journalism and sociology at New York University and author of* Sacrifice, *a novel.*

Where?

What is needed now is not a descendant of Edward R. Murrow, but rather someone who, like him, can invent a new journalistic idiom to exploit the technological advances available to bring home to America in a compelling way the most important stories of the day from outside its borders.—RICHARD HORNIK

Business News and International Reporting

*In a global economy, reporting that integrates business, poli-
tics and culture becomes ever more important.*

Richard Lambert

ONE OF THE most important business stories of the last 20 years was the
collapse of the Soviet Union. What seemed at the time like an event
primarily of political and strategic importance turned out to have profound consequences for financial markets and businesses everywhere.
It transformed the structure of Europe's most powerful economy, Ger-
many, in a way that was to have enormous consequences for all its
neighbors. Directly or indirectly, it opened the doors of countries around
the world that had previously been closed to foreign trade and international companies. It turned the United States into the unchallenged
global superpower and marked the start of a period in which the American brand of capitalism swept across the world.

Here's the paradox. Just as the old model of international news
reporting, based on bureaus of general correspondents, has moved into
a stage of rapid decline, so the business news organizations have been
expanding their networks of specialist correspondents around the world
at a hectic pace. While the television networks and big city newspapers were cutting back their foreign coverage and returning to base,
specialist groups like Reuters, Bloomberg, the Financial Times and
Dow Jones were—and still are—devoting an increasing share of their
resources to global news.

It's not just in the United States that the general public has become
more inward looking and less interested in what's happening elsewhere in the world. The same is happening in the United Kingdom

and the rest of Europe. It is also true that news organizations everywhere have become more concerned with maximizing profits and less interested in a public service function. Keeping expensive foreign bureaus has become increasingly hard to justify in the face of public indifference.

But in an increasingly globalized capital market, business news organizations have had to move in the opposite direction. As the Soviet collapse showed, political developments can have dramatic business consequences. And economic changes can have an equally big impact on politicians. The collapse of the banking system in Thailand in 1997 caused a chain reaction around the world. It helped to trigger political upheavals in South Korea and Indonesia. It tested the policies of Brazil's President Cardoso almost to the point of destruction. And its reverberations were felt not just in the financial markets of New York, London and Tokyo. They also rippled through the political capitals of the world.

Even the United States, for all its economic and strategic power, has become less immune to economic events outside its borders. International trade is accounting for an increasing share of its economy, and international trade conflicts have become a growing source of aggravation for its policy-makers. U.S. businesses have greatly increased their level of investment outside their own borders, and foreign companies have done the same within the United States. Portfolio investors have been putting significant sums in foreign bonds and equities. And the almighty dollar is facing its first real challenge in decades in the shape of the newly created Euro.

ALL THIS IS transforming the nature of business news reporting. It is not a coincidence that three of the leading international groups in this area are U.K. based—the Economist, Reuters and the Financial Times—because London has been the world's biggest international capital market for most of the last 200 years. But others are now following suit, and business reporters everywhere are having to take a broader view.

For example, the business pages in Detroit in the postwar decades really only had to be concerned with the performance of the big three automakers, which in turn was dictated by their own engineering and marketing skills, and by the strength of the domestic economy. But by the 1980s, these companies were facing serious threats from Japan, to the point where their very existence as volume manufacturers seemed in doubt. By the late 1990s, the story had shifted again. Now the story was about international alliances and takeovers. As Daimler merged with Chrysler, ambitious reporters in Detroit started to think about German lessons—and *The Detroit News* opened a bureau in Frankfurt. In a borderless business world, business correspondents can no longer stop at national boundaries.

Business news organizations need to have bureaus of reporters in international centers for a series of reasons. The most obvious is to cover spot news from important markets. Investors need a running commentary on what's happening in the financial exchanges of Tokyo or London, both because they own shares in those markets and because the way that prices and interest rates move there will influence trading in their own domestic centers. Business readers also need updates on the affairs of the big multinational companies. Who is forming alliances with whom across national borders? How is Sony adapting its strategies to an Internet world? And what opportunities will the deregulation of the telecommunications industry across Europe throw up for U.S. companies?

Business readers are looking for a context to help them understand events in their own marketplace. What is the reason for the prolonged fall in the price of oil, and what would trigger a change? Will the collapse of domestic demand in Japan make its companies a greater threat in international markets, or will it instead blunt their competitive edge? Will the Asian crisis be a good thing for the U.S. economy, by helping to damp down inflationary pressures, or will it pose greater competition for U.S. manufacturers and help to enlarge an already troubling trade deficit?

There are bigger, broader questions that also need reporting from the ground in a way that cannot be done by reporters who are passing through the region on a quick trip. China is the most obvious example. Its political and economic development over the next decade will have enormous implications for international security and trade, all of which will in turn bear directly on the business community. It is a difficult and complex story to report, one that requires an understanding of the subtlety and nuances of politics and culture as well as of the business community. The business news organization that does this best will have a distinct competitive edge and will certainly build its coverage on a platform of strong locally based reporting.

THIS EMPHASIS ON business as opposed to general news reporting is reconfiguring the landscape of international news. If you drew a map of the world on a scale that reflected the interests of a business readership, the United States would cover more than half the globe. The whole of sub-Saharan Africa might fit comfortably into New Jersey, and you would need a magnifying glass to find Bangladesh.

There are three problems here. The first is that business news organizations have a natural tendency to allocate their resources, both in terms of reporting and space, on the basis of a region's importance in terms of world trade or commodity output. This means that some international stories that are of great importance in strategic terms can get overlooked: Kosovo does not have a natural home on the business pages.

The second is that the priorities of these organizations will change in accordance with shifts in the global economy. In the wake of the OPEC oil boom in the 1970s, the *Financial Times* had a sizeable cadre of reporters devoted to the Middle East. This has been cut back over the years as the oil wealth was frittered away, and more firepower was required in Asia and Latin America. For a business audience, the region is less important than it was. But in terms of human and strategic interest, it remains of vital significance.

The third problem is that stock market movements and international trade flows are not the only guide to the kind of story that is going to matter to the business community, let alone to a broader audience. For example, there is no immediate reason why most businesspeople should care about events in North Africa. For all its natural resources, Algeria has been more or less shut off from the world by its domestic political troubles, and its neighbors to the west scarcely register on the global economic league tables. Yet the political and economic fortunes of North Africa are potentially of very direct economic interest to the whole of Western Europe. If things go badly in the region in the coming years, it is not difficult to imagine a tide of emigration that would pose great social and economic pressures across the Mediterranean.

It takes a longsighted news editor to recognize such issues. Business news reporters are also going to have to learn to ask questions that may not come naturally to people of their background and training. In Europe, for example, there is a broad consensus among the business community that the Economic and Monetary Union is the best way forward. But that view is not so widely spread among the community as a whole—and business leaders do not have a brilliant track record when it comes to judging such essentially political issues. Their consensus needs to be challenged and probed.

Indonesia is another example. Ahead of the economic and political crunch in 1997–98, it was widely regarded by business and suprana-tional organizations like the International Monetary Fund as a model Asian economy, and one that presented great business opportunities. Only later did it become clear that its structure had been undermined by corruption, financial imprudence and human rights abuses.

THE GROWTH OF global business news reporting helps to plug the gap left by the contraction of international reporting by television and general newspapers. Some publications, like *The Economist* and the *Financial Times* are deliberately seeking to reach out to a wider audi-ence, people who are not naturally readers of business news but who feel the need for a better understanding of what's going on outside their own country. But however successfully they do their job, busi-ness reporters in the end are going to be serving a rather narrow and exclusive audience.

One of the biggest challenges in the coming years will be to find ways of keeping the general public in touch with their place in the world. Sound political leadership depends on the support of informed citizens. That in turn requires a steady and consistent view of both local and international events—and one that is not just confined to the business pages.

Richard Lambert is editor of the Financial Times.

New Wars, New Correspondents

A shrinking world demands more international news, not less.

Stacy Sullivan

THE WORLD HAS been shrinking for a long time, but in the 1990s, with the proliferation of e-mail, international commerce and cheap travel, it is shrinking faster than ever before. The result is that faraway places become more relevant to our lives. There was a time when troubles in Indonesia would not have had an impact on our lives in the United States, but living in a global economy, the force of political and economic shocks in Asia reaches all the way to the United States. Today, when we can communicate several times a day with someone in Kazakhstan or Nepal by pressing a button, and when it is not unusual for some people to travel to different continents a few times a year, there is a greater likelihood that events in faraway places will shape our lives.

At the same time, the world has become messier. A decade ago, when the Soviet Union and the United States and their competing ideologies divided the world, international conflicts could always be shoehorned into a communist versus capitalist framework. The new conflicts unfolding around the world, however, are a variety of nationalist, religious and ethnic civil wars that have caught fire in complex, changing and unstable nations—places such as Bosnia, Rwanda, Kosovo and Sierra Leone—that find it difficult to contain different peoples in one polity. These conflicts have taken the lives of hundreds of thousands of people and have left millions more homeless and stateless. They have also produced a flood of wrenching and confounding visual images.

But pictures alone do not create understanding—that comes only with detailed reporting on the ground from people who can reconcile breaking news and historical context. And the news media are still obligated to cover distant places. Ethically and morally, it is repugnant to use ignorance as an excuse for ignoring vast regions of the world. Moreover, in an era of great immigration, international stories resonate with a larger number of Americans than is commonly assumed. Finally, for practical reasons, these stories are highly compelling— when they are related by a reporter with enough knowledge of the situation to make them clear.

It would seem logical that as events in foreign countries become both more relevant and more complex, news organizations would expand the number of foreign correspondents and foreign bureaus. Yet with the exception of the wire services and a few major newspapers, almost every news organization in the United States has cut back the number of foreign correspondents and foreign bureaus. The rationale, according to most editors and producers is simple: Americans aren't interested in foreign news. Moreover, covering foreign news is expensive. It makes bad business sense to spend significant amounts of money producing content that is not popular with readers and viewers. However, because the news media realize their professional obligations to cover these new conflicts despite their complexity and expense, they continue to do so. But not without compromise. Instead of using full-time staff correspondents, almost every American news organization, including *The New York Times*, has come to rely on local hires and stringers instead of staff correspondents to cover the world. Given the complexity, lack of public interest and cost related to foreign conflicts, it is extremely likely that news organizations will continue to do so in the future. I am one of those stringers, and in that sense I represent the future of foreign correspondents.

IN THE SPRING of 1995, I graduated from Columbia University's School of International and Public Affairs with a master's degree in international affairs and journalism. During my time in graduate school, I focused on Eastern Europe and passionately followed the breakup of Yugoslavia. I studied the history, politics and language of the region and longed to go there to cover the war. What aspiring journalist well versed in a region embroiled in war would not have felt the same? Were I to have gone the traditional route towards becoming a foreign correspondent—which would have entailed working at a small newspaper, moving on to a midsize paper, then eventually getting a position at a regional or national newspaper—it would have taken a minimum of five years to land an overseas position. That would have put me abroad in my early to mid-30s, just about the time I would want to settle down. Given my interests, my life goals and my expertise in a volatile region, I concluded it made more sense to go to Bosnia, and later Kosovo, while I was eager, single and young.

To my surprise, all of the news outlets I spoke with said they would be open to taking stories from me were I to go to Bosnia. Given what I now understand about the news media's reliance on stringers it doesn't surprise me, but at the time I was stunned. It seemed a crazy thing to do—run off to a war zone without any institutional backing. But I spoke with several free-lance journalists in the region, and they all assured me that there was plenty of work and that it wasn't that dangerous. It was with those hasty assurances, a borrowed flak jacket and a couple thousand dollars that I made my way to Sarajevo.

Once I arrived, I quickly discovered that there was a gang of free-lancers in the war zone. Among us, we covered the war in Bosnia for *Newsweek*, *Time*, *U.S. News & World Report*, *The Boston Globe*, *The Times* (London), the *Daily Telegraph*, the *Chicago Tribune*, *The Dallas Morning News* and the *Houston Chronicle*—all major news outlets that didn't have full-time foreign correspondents covering the region. All of these newspapers and magazines had staff correspondents, based in Rome, Vienna, Berlin or Warsaw, who would drop into the region from time to time, but the bulk of reporting was left to us—a corps of intelligent and hardworking twenty-somethings who shared a passion for the region and wanted to forge careers as foreign correspondents. The lack of any formal infrastructure from news organizations meant that we had to provide for ourselves. We rented apartments in several different cities in the former Yugoslavia—Zagreb, Sarajevo, Tuzla and Belgrade—and shared the rent. We lent one another cars and shared translators.

It was, in many ways, a mutually beneficial arrangement: the news organizations got an area covered at a discounted rate, and we got to cover a major international story for prestigious news organizations that we could have otherwise only dreamed of writing for. It was also an exploitative relationship that compromised both our safety and the quality of coverage the newspapers and magazines provided.

Not formally backed by news organization—many of us had con-tracts, but even these did not obligate the news organizations to give us medical insurance or ensure that we would be evacuated should we get injured—all of us were vulnerable to losing our positions on the whims of editors. We risked being left stranded should something have happened to us. Looking back, I can't help but marvel at how lucky my colleagues and I were that none of us was injured or killed.

Our indispensability to the news organizations, no doubt, was re-flected in the coverage we provided. When something particularly newsworthy happened, we found ourselves overstretched, often filing four or five stories each day—recycling quotes and differing each article only slightly. The number of deadlines meant we often had to cut short our reporting time—which no doubt affected the quality of our output. If we had had the security of a news organization behind us and had we been able to concentrate our efforts on one news outlet instead of several, our coverage, and thus that of the newspapers and magazines, would have been substantially more thorough. At the same time, we would not have had to take such substantial risks to our personal safety.

If we were staff correspondents, had anything happened to us, the news organization would have taken responsibility. For example, if I had been captured and detained by the Bosnian Serbs as a staff corre-spondent, *Newsweek* would have been on the phone to the State De-partment doing everything possible to secure my release. As a stringer, they did not have that responsibility. What they might have done on my behalf would have been at their own discretion.

GIVEN BOTH THE need for more foreign coverage and the economic impracticality of sending more correspondents overseas, is there any other compromise that could be reached that would minimize exploita-tion and maximize quality and breadth of coverage? I suggest that there is, but the solution requires a new way of thinking about foreign coverage.

The answer is to increase the number of correspondents in overseas bureaus by adding younger and thus cheaper journalists to the over-seas staff. The current mentality of magazine and newspaper editors—that future foreign correspondents must move up through the ranks, covering cops and local politics—is inappropriate for the state of a complicated and changing world. The reporting of refugee outflows, mass atrocities and natural disasters is no doubt aided by years of covering local stories—but not nearly to the extent that editors suggest. Regional expertise, experience overseas and linguistic abilities are every bit as valuable as, if not more than, domestic reporting experience.

If those who want to be foreign correspondents—well-traveled people with a talent for languages and an understanding of the complex new world order—had the possibility to get an overseas posting after waiting only a year or two, they would be much more inclined to get a staff job and put in the time it takes to become a staff foreign correspondent rather than taking extreme risks to pursue what they want to do. I know I would have. They would also be willing to earn substantially less than the senior correspondents who currently get overseas positions. And because of the reduced likelihood of younger correspondents having a family that would have to be established overseas, they would cost significantly less to relocate.

In short, editors need to open their minds to a new breed of foreign correspondent—younger, single and, by virtue of the latter two qualities, cheaper than the majority of correspondents currently being sent overseas by most news organizations. That way, media outlets could send more than one correspondent to a region, or keep more than one correspondent in a bureau at marginally higher costs.

If news organizations could increase the number of foreign correspondents in their bureaus, they could also avoid the mayhem and confusion that often accompany big international stories and provide more thorough information to foreign policy-makers as well. Currently, the press ignores many regions of the world until they become catastrophic. Once that happens, correspondents from all over the world parachute in, providing coverage that is erratic and ill informed. Kosovo is a case and point.

The latest battleground in a series of conflicts that have broken out in the former Yugoslavia, Kosovo was an obscure province before it became the biggest story in the world. It was left to be explained by reporters who knew little about it. Yet what happened there in the spring of 1999 was quite predictable.

In October 1998, even as the NATO alliance was threatening to bomb Yugoslavia, most news organizations continued to rely on local hires and stringers to cover the region. I was one of them. As I spoke to people in Kosovo's regional capital, Pristina, I heard the same fears over and over again: if NATO bombs without sending in ground troops, the Serbian population will take out recriminations on the Albanian civilians.

The urban intellectuals of Pristina predicted exactly the events of 1999 in Kosovo, yet very few news organizations reported these fears. I believe this kind of reporting could have swayed policy-makers not to leave the province's Albanian population vulnerable without ground forces or international monitors during NATO attacks, and I believe it could also have saved hundreds, if not thousands, of lives.

Sadly, I have seen the future of foreign reporting—it is Kosovo. I can only hope that the system by which the American news media covers the world will be reformed.

Stacy Sullivan covered the war in bosnia for Newsweek *and the Kosovo conflict for* The New York Times Magazine. *She is currently a consultant to Harvard University's Human Rights Initiative.*

A Web of Sound

The fruitful convergence of radio, audio and the Internet

Kenneth R. Donow and Peggy Miles

THE VERY CONCEPT of radio rests on some facts of physics. Modulate the electromagnetic spectrum. Push your product—your signal—into the physical world so that large numbers of people in your expected coverage area can acquire the signal with their home radios. Once the signal is processed, the listener has your program. It's become a routine matter, a good reliable way of transferring information from a single, central point to a very large number of listeners.

Yet radio, like so many other media, is being transformed by its encounter with the Internet. The Internet has provided a medium for the transmission of sound files so robust, potent and flexible as to make the entire system of radio that we now take for granted into something so completely different as to be revolutionary. The most obvious difference is that the transfer of radio programming from source to listeners no longer depends on the critical infrastructure of broadcasting, most importantly on radio waves. Now, radio becomes Internet audio. With Internet audio, any radio program can be broadcast live on the Net or replayed at any time. Listeners will be able to hear instantly any program from anywhere in the world. These capacities will give Internet audio an appeal transcending that of radio.

But to grow, the cost of receiving Internet radio signals must get cheaper, and the receivers must become more portable. In contrast, radios simply do not cost very much. The prices range from a couple of dollars at the low end to a few hundred at the very highest. Of course, specialized radios—such as desktop shortwave and ham systems—can cost quite a bit more than that, but the number of these radios are relatively few. Also, radio is portable. As with any other form of electronic equipment, radios have become much smaller over the past 25 years. A vast number of features are packed into a single device. Even shortwave radios, with complex digital tuning and memories, plus standard antennae and power interfaces, are now smaller than a trade paperback book.

As a result of these factors, radio is ubiquitous. There is more than one radio per person in most of the industrialized world. In the developing world the radio density is quite high by any measure: in the poorest countries in the world, where the radio density is approximately 20 percent, there is a large amount of out-of-home and group listening.

There are, however, some limitations to radio. Radio can only be useful if the signals put out by broadcasters can be received. That sounds like more simple a matter than it is, in fact. Without support of something like a satellite delivery system bringing FM subcarriers to satellite dishes and cable head ends, FM signals have a limited reach of approximately 100 miles. Medium wave signals can go quite a bit farther in ideal propagation circumstances, well more than 1,000 miles. Shortwave signals can be unstable in the most ideal circumstances, but they are capable of delivering radio for many thousands of miles.

THE ENCOUNTER BETWEEN radio and the Internet raises transforming possibilities. The Internet adds some wonderful capabilities to radio in that it eliminates the propagation constraints imposed on radio broadcasting. Indeed, it may be helpful to forget the notion of radio at all, because it is so tied to the physical properties of the radio spectrum, and substitute the concept of audio or audio information.

The Internet is the most global medium. It brings radio from any broadcaster in the world to anyone anywhere who wants to listen to the program. For example, someone sitting in Washington, D.C. with a modest Internet connection has instant access to live programming from Ghana, Singapore, Hong Kong and Australia. Still, the full international potential of sound on the Internet has not yet been realized.

As one might expect, most of the world's Webcasters are radio stations. However, there are signs of Internet audio becoming a medium in its own right. Of the more than 2,000 Webcasters making programming available to the worldwide Internet, 8 percent distribute their programming exclusively on the Internet.

For the international broadcasters—VOA, BBC, Deutsche Welle—Internet audio is a medium consistent with their responsibilities to bring as much objective and balanced news and current affairs information to as many of the world's listeners as possible. Internet audio may mean something different for local stations with news operations. For one thing, they can point to news listeners they capture as new audiences and argue with advertisers that the rates they charge for publicity on the new medium should be correspondingly higher. From the vantage point of people who seek a wide range of news sources on the radio, news reports issuing over the Internet from local markets around the world will become a new and valued first source of information on many stories of critical concern. For example, anyone seeking firsthand coverage of a trial with important political ramifications in Malaysia—the trial of deposed deputy prime minister Anwar Ibrahim, an event that sparked wide protests in his country—could find real-time, on-the-ground reporting over the Internet from RTM (the Malaysian state broadcaster), RCS (the Radio Corporation of Singapore) and Radio Australia.

To UNDERSTAND FULLY the near and midterm future of radio on the Internet, it helps to think about the problem in two steps. First, the merger of the Internet with radio will occur on familiar grounds using devices already in existence. For example, audio compression schemes will have to become a bit better to stand in for uncompressed, over-the-air radio distribution. As good as they are, present schemes such as MPEG 3, a standard for the compression of audio information, are pretty good for the Internet but not that good when compared to the sound qualities of uncompressed FM. Second is the refinement of interface technologies linking the net to devices such as your television or stereo. Because this is essentially the same software problem at work in linking the different components of a desktop personal computer system, it is probably an easier problem to solve.

Eventually, all programming and content will be created in fully digitized studios. Programming now distributed over traditional broadcast media will be distributed using digital techniques and acquired and then viewed or otherwise consumed over digital television sets or devices such as Audible, Diamond Rio and MP3 replay instruments. FM (frequency modulated) and AM (amplitude modulated) radio spectrum will then have given way to audio bit streams. The consequences of the full digitization of this process are yet to be known. However, we can be pretty certain that all media content distributed over the traditional broadcast media will appear on-line. Niche channels will appear, and each program provider presently operating as a radio station will have multiple Webcast stations, providing content for the Internet only. Audio bit streams will merge with other types of output devices such as digital TVs.

The next steps presumed in the process of bringing the revolution in Internet audio to full term focus on wireless portability. First, we can expect handheld computers to be multimedia capable, able to acquire and process text, audio and video files. Second, the handheld, portable Internet replay instrument—a radio or a wireless audio device—will interface to the global telecommunications network much like the new satellite telephone systems (such as ICO, Globalstar or Iridium), permitting listeners to pick up stations outside their coverage areas.

Digital audio devices with global reach certainly change the definition of a media market. No longer will local radio stations be able to force-feed shrinking pop playlists to captive audiences. Instead, listeners interested in jazz will have a global choice of radio stations to capture their attention. When these devices interface to the Internet, the choice of programming escapes the constraints of national boundaries.

At some point, these devices will be every bit as interactive as present desktop computers. They will be connected to the worldwide Internet wireless telecommunications infrastructure so that users—first professionals and later the general public—can interact with each other through horizontal exchanges of information and complement the vertical transfer of information from broadcasters to listeners.

WHILE THE FULL consequences of the blending of radio and the Internet are still ahead of us, in the recent history of war in the Balkan states of the former Yugoslavia we can glimpse the future of international radio on the Internet. A few years ago, the Serbian regime attempted to close down Radio B92, the sole independent radio broadcaster in the capital city Belgrade. Prior to Internet radio, this would have been a relatively simple matter. A strategically placed radio jammer broadcasting signals on the same frequency as B92 would have made the station impossible to listen to.

B92 made an effective counterattack. In addition to using loudspeakers and bull horns from their office windows to broadcast news to crowds marching through the streets of Belgrade protesting the reversal of local elections, an alliance of human rights groups in Europe plus a number of international broadcasters supported B92's using the Internet to come back on air.

Supported by the Amsterdam-based Internet site XS4ALL, B92 fed a digitized version of their broadcasts to the site http://www.xs4all.net, which was then interfaced to the broadcast facilities of a number of international broadcasting organizations (VOA, RFE and BBC) who then beamed the signal back to Belgrade. That particular battle in the Balkan information war was won easily by the opposition. The Yugoslavian government quickly stood down, and B92 returned to air more or less uninterrupted until the current campaign.

B92 has been thought by some observers to have fallen victim to the Yugoslavian government during the present NATO-Serbian conflict over the future of Kosovo. At the beginning of the conflict, B92 was the primary opposition source of on-the-ground reporting—audio and video—from Belgrade. Some onlookers have expressed the belief that B92 has succumbed to threats and is self-censoring its reports. Whether or not that is the case, the worst that can be concluded is that the station may have lost this battle, but there can be no question that the war is not yet over. Other providers of information with sources on the ground in Kosovo and in the rest of the region—such as the Institute for War and Peace Reporting, the Kosova Crisis Center and the Alternative Information Network in former Yugoslavia—are reporting important details of the present conflict to the rest of the world.

The genie is out of the bottle. Desktop computers are the new studios for the production of audio and video information; with them, anyone can become an Internet broadcaster. While their link to the worldwide Internet may be vulnerable to censors in the short term, suppressing Internet transmission is easier said than done. With the coming of cheap wireless connections to the Internet using global satellite telephony, efforts to block the transmission of sound over the Internet will become all the more complicated, expensive and, eventually, fruitless.

Kenneth R. Donow is a media researcher based in Washington, D.C. Peggy Miles is president of Intervox Communications and author of Internet Age Broadcaster.

Why?

The whole world is speeding up so rapidly that you don't need to fear that people are not going to get enough of it. What we need to fear is that they don't get enough time to sit quietly and read good books and to think about journalistic subjects historically, culturally—to see a subject through these other lenses that give good journalism real depth and resonance.—ORVILLE SCHELL

New News, New Ideas

Deans explore the challenges of educating the journalists of the future.

Interviews with David Rubin, Orville Schell, Ken Bode, Geoffrey Cowan,
Terry Hynes, Robert Ruggles and Tom Goldstein

Compiled by Jennifer Kelley

IN OCTOBER *1998, Marvin Kalb, director of the Joan Shorenstein Center on the Press, Politics and Public Policy and Edward R. Murrow Professor of the Press and Public Policy at the John F. Kennedy School of Government, Harvard University, issued a discussion paper: The Rise of the "New News": A Case Study of Two Root Causes of Modern Scandal Coverage. Kalb concluded that American journalism has "lost the trust and confidence of so many of its readers and viewers" not because of a collapse in professional standards, but because of new challenges posed by technology and the economic restructuring of the news industry. "Both of these challenges have forced a revolutionary transformation of the news business from a public service into a predominately commercial enterprise, where profit tends to trump service at just about every bend in the road. The effect has been to change the very definition of journalism and to produce a 'new news.'"*

Is there a new news? And if there is, how should educators prepare the next generation of journalists for their encounter with this rough beast? Jennifer Kelley put these questions and more to the deans of schools of journalism and communications around the United States. Here is a sampling of their answers.

111

David Rubin

David Rubin is dean of the S.I. Newhouse School of Communications
at Syracuse University.

MSJ: *Given the new pressures affecting journalism, what are the prospects of journalism education?*
David Rubin: One of the things that has changed the most is that there are now many more players in the news business than there used to be. Technology has made it possible for people all over the country to gain access to those players, whether it is by cable or broadcasting or national distribution of newspapers or the Internet or whatever.

On the national scene there are many more players than there used to be. And this has changed the economics of the business because it has fragmented the audience, which has impacted advertising and sales. That has added a competitive dimension to the news business that didn't exist 30 years ago. And to the extent that this relentless competition has taken its toll on the news business, I guess you could say it has meant, however you want to put it, a change in standards, a change in the definitions of news, or a lowering of standards. I think that is true generally speaking, because everybody is involved in this competition, but it is not true in some of our leading news organizations. I do not accept that the standards at *The New York Times* or *The Washington Post* have changed.

When you are looking at specialized kinds of information—whether it is business, financial, cultural—and you are looking at publications that deal with those narrower niches, one could argue that there has never been more valuable information in niches ever before. It is a much richer news diet. And I also think it is fair to say that if as an American today you want to be informed, it is much easier to be informed now than it was 30 years ago. There is certainly no excuse for an American to say, "I didn't know," or, "I am only getting my news from one source and they misled me."

Overall, the picture is rather brighter than it was 30 years ago. I am a big believer in competition, and I think that the increasing nichification of the media is not bad. I think it is good.
MSJ: *How can this competitive environment affect journalism education?*
David Rubin: We prepare them by making certain they understand

what the media environment is, through an introductory lecture or seminar course about the media in America, so that they are not naive about it. But quite frankly in much of the instruction I don't think the competition issue is relevant. I still think that to make good journalists you have to teach them how to get information and where to get information and then what do with that information once they have it. I think it is really both as simple and as complicated as that.

MSJ: *In your experience, how does the new media environment really affect the journalism school environment and curriculum processes?*

David Rubin: It affects it budgetarily, in that you have to start setting aside money for the purchase of computer hardware, software and, most expensive, ongoing computer support personnel, which you didn't have to do a decade ago. Given what I said about where to find information and how to evaluate information, there are now many more places to go for information than there used to be, which you have got to build into the curriculum. In training reporters we need to teach them what all those places are and to evaluate what it is they're getting, since not all information is equal. And that makes things more complicated than they were 10 or 15 years ago.

MSJ: *Implicit in what you are saying is that one of the emerging purposes of journalism education is that of not only supplying information, but filtering and evaluating it. What goals then do you think journalism education should seek to achieve?*

David Rubin: It is a different world from earlier times when a journalist's main information-gathering technique was the interview. The interview is still important—and one still needs to teach journalists how to use that tool—but there are many more things. We need to teach the use of the computer as an investigative tool, either to do number crunching or to reveal patterns in behavior, or to search the World Wide Web for additional data. And we need to explain to students how one evaluates information. What is a good source? How can you tell if information is reliable and valid?

It used to be when you were interviewing the question was, who are you interviewing and what was their position in life and how well do you know them and what is their track record, and so on. We need new rules for these new types of information. I think everybody is struggling, deciding how much time we can devote to this sort of instruction, but it is important to do.

MSJ: *What kind of ethos or sense of purpose should journalism education instill in the students that it sends out into the profession?*
David Rubin: We still have to make them excited about being the public's eyes and ears, about being an essential part of the American democratic process, about representing the voiceless and the underdog, about being an adversary or at least a watchdog of power and about recognizing that they are in this business not for the money but for the contribution they make to the overall health of the country. And that I don't think has changed at all—or it should not have changed.

Orville Schell

Orville Schell is dean of the Graduate School of Journalism at the University of California, Berkeley.

MSJ: *Do you think that we are incorrect in assuming that the future of journalism looks bleak, so to speak?*
Orville Schell: What is so confusing is that there are some very encouraging examples, and there are also a fairly large number of very discouraging examples. So it is a little bit hard to know what the trend will ultimately be. But clearly the marketplace has made a massive inroad into the whole dynamic of media outlets of every kind. It used to be that there were places that were a little more protected from the sweeps-week mentality. But those preserves are really being overrun. That is quite an alarming turn of events.

From the perspective of being the dean of a journalism school, I should say that once I really did wonder if journalism schools had any function. Why go to a school when you can just get out there and get into the belly of the beast and learn as a good apprentice learns from a shoemaker?

But I think the point to be made now is that most media outlets no longer have these lower rungs on the ladder that can pull members of the younger generation up through the training process. Given the marketization of the media and the competition for profitability in most media outlets, this seems like a waste of resources. The editor of one very big and reputable daily said to me, "We don't train people, we cherry pick five or six years out."

Such a changed situation does, I think, build the case for a good hands-on journalism school, where younger people can do journalism but at the same time get the kind of editorial help, the kind of technical help and some of the handholding of a master-apprentice relationship that has vanished at most media outlets. We don't have the copy boy ending up as editor any longer because there are no more copy boys. There are some internships, but they comprise a very spotty kind of institution.

MSJ: *What should be the purpose of journalism education?*

Orville Schell: What journalism schools have to start being is something like baseball farm teams. The best way to feed into the big leagues is for people to actually play ball. I think journalism schools really have to find ways to partner with real media outlets. But I think this is something that first-rate media outlets—whether ABC Television, the *Los Angeles Times*, *The New Yorker*, whatever—have not fully embraced.

MSJ: *What is the ethos or sense of purpose that you want to instill in your students, through their course work, about their profession?*

Orville Schell: Our challenge is to inoculate students with a sense of journalistic ethics, excellence and a kind of confidence that they know how to accomplish those ends. This is not simply gained, I think, by listening to sermons. It is gained by watching other people do it. It is absorbed by being around credible, ethical, serious and excellent practitioners of the craft.

This is the way I learned. When I was a graduate student here at Berkeley, a professor asked me to help him do a book, and we ended up co-authoring three books together. Then at *The New Yorker*, I had a series of extraordinary editors who worked with me for weeks, sometimes for five or six hours a day, on a single piece. And I saw how the editing process evolved. I saw what one could do if one took the time with an integral relationship with a good editor. This is what we need to replicate at journalism schools. Journalists don't just spring forth without some incubation.

MSJ: *How do you prepare students to confront the pressures of 24-hour news on the Internet and an accelerated news cycle?*

Orville Schell: Well, this is a Cyclops that is catching us all up in its fury. Fortunately, we are a two-year program, not a one-year program. Two years is still not enough time, but it allows us to get students to read some great works of nonfiction, to think a bit, to establish some fund of basic knowledge about the field—to learn about what has gone before, about what is good writing, filmmaking and broadcasting. It is a kind of undertaking that will be very hard for anyone to do once they are out in the trade in this high-speed world, buffeted by around-the-clock competition.

The whole world is speeding up so rapidly that you don't need to fear that people are not going to get enough of it. What we need to fear is that they don't get enough time to sit quietly and read good books and to think about journalistic subjects historically, culturally—to see a subject through these other lenses that give good journalism real depth and resonance.

I think speed is coming quite naturally to us, and we can't avoid it. It is threatening to melt everybody. The best antidote is reading and reflecting.

My current thinking is that taking a little more time before you get thrown into the outside centrifuge can only arm you better in terms of knowing how to do the kind of journalism that will be credible and well thought of—and how to keep your balance in this incredibly high-speed, competitive world, where the market is pecking at one every minute.

There are very few jobs that are perfect—but I think the challenge for young journalists is to know how to negotiate in a world where compromise will be asked of them more often than not.

Young journalists increasingly need resistance to maintain standards and their own sense of excellence in this very competitive and market-driven world.

Ken Bode

Ken Bode is dean of the Medill School of Journalism
at Northwestern University.

MSJ: *What are the prospects of journalism education—is there cause for worry or for optimism?*
Ken Bode: I think the widely reported breakdown of journalistic standards is vastly overstated. Over the past year, a very difficult major story developed involving sex between the president and a White House intern, followed by lies and a cover-up. On the one hand it was tawdry in its essence, and on the other hand it always had the potential to have the highest possible consequences for the country.

A great deal of privacy was blown up on all sides, not because of the press in most cases, but mostly because of the independent counsel—and because of the nature of the story.

Many of the critics of journalism who rushed to condemn the leaks and single-source journalism and so forth turned out to be quite wrong in their premises. In time, serious studies showed very little of that. They would run on to television and talk about a failure of respected news organizations to abide by double sourcing in the newsroom. As moderator of "Washington Week in Review," I would ask reporters like David Broder of *The Washington Post* and bureau chiefs like Doyle McManus of the *Los Angeles Times* and Alan Murray of *The Wall Street Journal* and Michael Duffy of *Time* magazine, to name just a few, what their standards were in the newsroom. And they all said, "Are you crazy? Do you think at a time like this when everybody is watching us so carefully that we are going to abandon our professional standards?"

So I think a lot of it was overstated by the critics. There are a lot of people who will rush to go on television just to be on television, and I think some of our prominent media critics fall right into that category.

MSJ: *As the dean of a journalism school, how do you prepare your students and help them understand their sense of purpose?*

Ken Bode: The first thing I do is explain to them that many of the people who have set themselves up as great authorities on the quality of journalism are a little quick on the draw. If they just checked, they would find out that their own perceptions or their own charges were very difficult to substantiate.

Second, any time you have things like *The Boston Globe* episode, the CNN episode or *The Cincinnati Enquirer* episode and so forth, these are teachable moments in journalism. [*Editor's note:* The episode involved a published investigation of Chiquita Banana, which the *Enquirer* retracted. The *Enquirer* also paid $10 million in damages to Chiquita and the reporter on the story plead guilty to illegally breaking into Chiquita's computer system and using its e-mail in reporting the story.] You have to take students beyond the fact that in *The Cincinnati Enquirer* episode there were very questionable techniques used by the reporter and make them understand the power of the enterprise being investigated in Cincinnati and the fact that we still don't really know all that happened in that story. The same thing is true of Tailwind at CNN. Some people may be sure they know that the story has no truth in it, but I am not so sure.

Basically, we have a tendency to wear a hair shirt right now. Food Lion: you've got to tell them both sides of that case. You've got to teach ethics in the present atmosphere, and you've got to teach it hard. But it's not all negative.

I try to have as much contact directly with both undergraduate and graduate students as I can and ask them, What do we do well here and what is it that you think we could do better?

Medill has a Washington newsroom, and I went there one night and bought 10 pizzas for our students, and we sat there for two and a half hours. The one thing that I will never forget is a young woman who said to me, "You know, when I was a sophomore in high school I knew that all I ever wanted to be was a journalist, and I haven't changed." But, she said, "I leave here feeling a little empty and with a little bit of a hangover, because you guys taught us so much about what was wrong in journalism and you never showed us what was really great about journalism."

We are hiring senior people in broadcasting and Internet journalism, and I say to them: "I want you to be on my team about this. We are going to make these kids leave here inspired."

MSJ: *What should the purpose and goals of journalism education be?*
Ken Bode: I think about it in this way: stand out there 10 years from now and look back and try to anticipate the challenges that our students are going to face in the first 10 years of the new millennium, in terms of the rapid technological changes, in terms of what I think is a reversible decline in public trust about journalism and a convergence of all of the technologies. We are in the strongest sense a truly converging profession, and our students have got to understand that.

We are refashioning the entire first quarter of our graduate degree program so we can also then acquaint them with what we call the environment of journalism—what has happened as large corporations have bought up newspapers, as chains have bought up independent newspapers, as afternoon dailies have gone out of business, as magazine companies like Meredith Corp. in Des Moines have moved from magazines to television as well.

If you step out of journalism school with a master's degree, and you don't understand the economic environment of journalism, and you don't understand what it meant to ABC News when ABC was bought by CAP Cities and then CAP Cities sold out to Disney—then you haven't gotten full value for your master's degree.

MSJ: *Given that these students are going to go out into this environment, with what ethos or sense of purpose do you really want to send them out?*

Ken Bode: Journalism students come to school for a lot of different reasons. I don't want to make it seem too pedestrian, but I don't know that everybody has the same sort of loftiness to their goals. Some come only to get a good job—and that's a good reason.

What I want them to have when they leave is a solid professional sense of what journalism is about. And the solid skills they need to perform it, whether they are Internet journalists or producers in broadcasting, reporters in broadcasting, whether they are in print, magazine writers, long form and so forth. I want them to be skilled writers. I want them to know the difference between what is a proven fact and what is still unproven.

I want all those basics, but if I had to say one thing that I also want, I hope they leave with a sense of how much fun they are going to have reporting to a different location every day and having the right to ask everybody questions about what goes on in the world. What a joy it is not to have to report to the same office every day, and what a joy it is to go out there and be able to see the world in front of you and say, "All of it is available to me to be examined." That is what I really think a journalist ought to know, given that we are not going to be paid very much—that you just can't have more fun.

Geoffrey Cowan

Geoffrey Cowan is dean of the Annenberg School for Communication at the University of Southern California.

Mid-career education is becoming more and more prevalent in practically all fields. For journalists it becomes important in a couple of ways. First of all, because there is a burnout factor that people are finding, and it provides an opportunity to get refreshed and restarted. Secondly, technologies change, specializations develop and values are under assault, and it gives people a chance to re-educate or newly educate themselves. And, of course, one of the great things about journalists is they are inherent learners. They are curious—that is why they become journalists, and that makes them wonderful students.

Terry Hynes

Terry Hynes is dean of the School of Journalism at the University of Florida.

Journalism has a very public purpose in helping people understand the world around them so they can better govern themselves. That may sound overly idealistic: I don't really want to apologize for it—it is how I maintain my optimism.

Robert Ruggles

Robert Ruggles is dean of the School of Journalism at Florida A&M University.

We simply have got to do a better job of instilling in our students what the values and standards and ethics of journalism are and should be.

Tom Goldstein

Tom Goldstein is dean of the Graduate School of Journalism at Columbia University.

I would hope people don't go into journalism to be famous.

Gnats Chasing an Elephant

*Press criticism grounded in the public interest has yielded to
media criticism that seeks consumer satisfaction.*

James Boylan

THE TERMS OF press criticism remain unsettled. We have a rough understanding of how to criticize, say, a book, a play or a restaurant, but
there has never been a consensus on the forms or bounds of criticism
of journalism, which is, after all, not a single artistic creation but a
complex social institution—a major actor in politics, an industry with
units ranging in scale from global to local, a technologically diverse
product that blankets the nation every day and a fluid profession or
quasi-profession with its own embedded traditions and culture. The
scope of the enterprise is so much greater than the available critical
range that in pessimistic moments I think of press critics as a mere
cloud of gnats trying to keep up with a galloping elephant, which
neither slows down nor turns right or left as it crashes through the
underbrush. It is never certain whether critics can get the beast's attention, let alone train it to do useful work.

Yet press criticism has been persistently on hand for almost as long
as the press itself; it continues today and those of us who have tried to
contribute to it have been customarily convinced that it serves good
purposes. Yet as we approach a new century we have become less
certain that we are doing good, less certain of our agenda, less certain
of appropriate forms. The time may be at hand for unblinking re-
evaluation.

PRESENT PRESS CRITICISM has grown out of its past. Much of it has resembled the characterization by the historian Allan Nevins of newspaper clipping morgues—"jumbled, disparate and trivial." But some is worth recalling. In the century's early decades, muckrakers held sway: Will Irwin and Charles Edward Russell attacked petty corruption and shaky ethics. They were succeeded by Upton Sinclair, who invoked a brothel artifact (*The Brass Check*, 1920) to imply press prostitution; Silas Bent, who criticized the tabloidization of the 1920s in *Ballyhoo* (1927); and George Seldes, who detected totalitarian sympathies among American press lords. Heavy-duty thinkers such as Walter Lippmann (*Liberty and the News*, 1920) deplored the buckling of journalism's integrity under pressures of war and politics.

A semblance of continuity arrived in the 1930s with *The New Yorker*'s "The Wayward Press," written first by Robert Benchley, then by A.J. Liebling, who ridiculed the sometimes stuffy and self-deluding folkways of journalism. (The feature died with Liebling.) The newsmagazines also had weekly press departments, but at midcentury the American printed press and its broadcast siblings had to put up with only sporadic criticism. So unaccustomed were publishers to unkind words that as late as 1960, the mere title of Carl E. Lindstrom's mild book, *The Fading American Newspaper*, caused a minor scandal.

But in the '60s, journalism was transformed in a confluence of historical circumstances: the growing visibility, prosperity and apparent dominance of the media, particularly television, in American life; the urgency and complexity of dealing with the decade's crises—the civil rights uprising, the Vietnam War, radical political drama, the arrival of a postwar generation of journalists. The shopworn press began its transformation into the more glamorous array called news media; what had been merely an ill-paid line of work turned into something resembling a profession with a semblance of professional standards.

Like it or not, those who ran journalism soon faced a steady and increasing diet of criticism. At first the efforts were, as Nevins said, disparate: a monthly communications supplement in *Saturday Review* magazine, weekly critiques from CBS-owned television stations and the *Columbia Journalism Review*, founded in 1961 at Columbia University's Graduate School of Journalism under Dean Edward W. Barrett. (I was its editor in the 1960s and again in the late 1970s.) As the decade heated up, the unruly alternative press also took shots at establishment media.

The year 1968 opened the gates. After the tumultuous Democratic convention, Chicago journalists seized the name "journalism review" for a new kind of alternative publication in which journalists criticized the media that employed them. Despite the obvious vulnerability of such enterprises, the new "reporter power" reviews spread across the country—Philadelphia, Houston, Twin Cities, West Coast. Many did not last long, but their freshness and frankness left a mark.

The publication that best embodied the spirit of the short-lived movement was *[More]*, founded in New York under Richard Pollak, with help from the Pulitzer Prize-winners J. Anthony Lukas and David Halberstam. It invoked the charismatic name of A.J. Liebling in designating its "counter-convention," staged opposite the spring publishers' rituals; at the meetings, it honored such irritants to the establishment as the dissident I.F. Stone and the skeptical reporter Homer Bigart.

To a degree, *[More]* and the other reviews were set up in opposition to what they believed the *Columbia Journalism Review* and other academe-based efforts signified—tame, stuffy press criticism, issued from a distance and from on high. In contrast, *[More]* offered criticism as serious fun and determined irreverence. However, in 1978, *[More]* was ignominiously folded into *CJR*, which continues to this day—as does *CJR*'s double, the *Washington* (now *American*) *Journalism Review*.

BUT THE OLDER journalism reviews were not destined to dominate the field. By the 1980s, the general press began to recognize the media as a major news subject. Where once coverage of journalism in newspapers might have consisted of fawning stories on publishers' meetings, now newspapers and magazines assigned reporters to media stories. A few newspapers appointed internal critics, ombudsmen, charged with analyzing issues involving their own operations (such as the 1981 report of *The Washington Post* ombudsman on Janet Cooke's calamitous faked Pulitzer Prize story). A scattering of news organizations also cooperated in the creation of the National News Council, a quasi-judicial complaints board whose reports were interred in the back pages of *CJR*.

Enhanced exposure at least laid media issues before the public, but it did not necessarily produce stronger or deeper criticism. News media did not often publish criticism as such but handled journalism as they handled other topics by putting it into convenient containers—sometimes as business news, occasionally as exposés, frequently as gossip, increasingly as celebrity chatter and invariably as a comet's tail to political stories, as has been the case with the Clinton scandals.

Meanwhile, other formats, critical and quasi-critical, have emerged. Radio and television critiques—of which "Reliable Sources," the weekly program on CNN anchored by Howard Kurtz of *The Washington Post* and Bernard Kalb, is the most recent and substantial—have been added to the mix, as has the appearance of media-discussion sites on-line, some of them offshoots of old publications, others in increasing numbers designed specifically for the Internet.

In the broad view, this continued expansion of possible channels for criticism must be seen as a gain. But it is of course not good news for the surviving journalism reviews. Essentially nonpartisan, if with liberal leanings, they have long since ceded the wide field of political analysis of the media to such organizations on the right and left as the long-lived Accuracy in Media (AIM) and Fairness and Accuracy in Reporting (FAIR). Their remaining options are restricted—to pursue the route of the specialized magazine, with the danger of becoming part of the trade press, or to compete for media stories with the general press in the hope of attracting a broader audience.

At *CJR*, at least, I know that the dream of turning a minuscule periodical into an *Atlantic Monthly* of journalism—a magazine appealing to a broad intellectual audience—dates from the 1970s. In recent years, both *CJR* and *American Journalism Review* have seemed to me to look less like magazines of criticism and more like general magazines that happen to deal with journalism.

But they have lacked a popular touch. In Steven Brill, the idea of a full-scale magazine about the media may have found the aggressive entrepreneur it required. *Brill's Content*, the bulky new monthly, strikes me as brilliantly attuned to this moment in press criticism. *Brill's Content*, in its own words, sees its reader as the "information consumer." It invokes an ethic of consumerism under which individual choice is applied to media output, just as it would be to choices of restaurants, movies or vacations. A degree of individual satisfaction, it is implied, may be gained by favoring one pundit over another, one search engine over another, one television news celebrity over another. Indeed, the magazine convened a focus group to help the viewer choose the morning network news program that fitted best with household routines. It is yet to be seen whether this appeal can attract a continuing audience, but it acutely strips from media criticism most public values.

TRADITIONALLY, CRITICISM OF journalism, dating back to the muckrakers, has invoked a criterion of the public interest or public good. Such standards are implied in *Brill's Content*, but so dimly as to be almost invisible. By thus reducing criticism of journalism to consumer choice, the magazine, and many of the other forms of media coverage and chatter available, confronts us with the question of whether journalism criticism is becoming useless in a public context. What purpose does criticism of journalism really serve, or what purpose ought it to serve?

These are not easy questions. Just as the muckrakers generally believed that the value of their work lay in exposure and that the solutions would take care of themselves, much criticism of journalism has assumed that pointing out flaws will lead to corrections. In a narrow sense, the purpose is thus reform. But it is hard to try to pin down even one reform attributable to critics of the press. More likely, the positive gains, if any, have come indirectly, with the media displaying a gradually growing reciprocity, a willingness to listen and to respond.

In the great end-of-century buzz of media talk, coverage, gossip and glamorization, however, it is not clear that basic, useful critical work is getting done or having good effect. Let us put the question this way: What critics' voices were heard consistently and clearly on the journalistic collapse of 1998, when news values bent and broke under Monican pressure; when news organizations hoodwinked the public by covertly playing unidentified-source games with the special prosecutor; when much of the press hastily joined in the hue-and-cry for terminating Clinton on the basis of then untested accusations?

What journalism criticism lacks, first, is critics of standing—capable writers who are willing to turn their hand consistently to press issues. In the past, there was at least a scattering of press critics of the "public intellectual" type, writers capable of commanding professional respect and public attention on a wide range of topics. Lippmann and Liebling were such figures, of dramatically antithetical types; more recently, Ben H. Bagdikian, who concentrated on media monopolies but covered many other topics, and Fred W. Friendly, who commented on ethical and First Amendment issues, commanded similar respect.

But too many possible candidates have burrowed into academic car-rels or moved on to other pastimes. It is indicative of the state of affairs that no major magazine or newspaper that I am aware of has a full-time press critic (as opposed to reporter or columnist). David Shaw at the *Los Angeles Times* and Howard Kurtz have been the closest thing.

But an even greater lack is the absence of an understood agenda. If press criticism can form coherent objectives, it probably can attract its writers. There is still important work to be done—not because critics can necessarily bring about specific change but because they can help frame the agenda around important issues of two types:

The first are social questions, asking whether journalism is building or eroding our society, whether it is politically constructive or destruc-tive, whether its procedures and organization are appropriate in a soci-ety that styles itself democratic, whether in short it is doing for society what it ought to do.

The second are questions on the conduct and practice of journalists, ethical and intellectual—whether journalists are acting intelligently, responsibly and ethically in the larger sense, as opposed to the obser-vance of petty restrictions on their private conduct.

These two types may seem to imply the segregation of criticism into inside and outside schools. Not necessarily so, for the objectives overlap. In the one case, criticism on larger social questions should provide ways for both citizens and journalists to think intelligently about an important institution in their society; in the other, criticism should offer ways for journalists to think intelligently about their work and for citizens to learn more about the nature of that work. Both forms should be framed in general, comprehensible and unspecialized language.

IN THE LAST year or two, there have been strenuous efforts to reorient a journalism that many see as crumbling before entertainment values and the technological maw. The Committee of Concerned Journalists has issued a call to colleagues to forswear sensation and "infotainment" and return to "traditional moorings." The allied Project for Excellence in Journalism, supported by the Pew Charitable Trusts, seeks "to clarify and raise the standards of American journalism." The American Soci-ety of Newspaper Editors has undertaken a "Journalism Credibility Project," while the Freedom Forum has launched a "Free Press, Fair

Press" initiative. What is notable about these efforts is their tradition-
alism, particularly their appeal to standards enunciated 52 years ago in
the report of the Commission on Freedom of the Press (the Hutchins
Commission).

What is wrong with that? When it was issued, the Hutchins report
irked journalists because it hinted that government might some day
step in to tame the press. But now other aspects of the report have
gained relevance because journalism is again, seemingly, facing the
vacuum in values that inspired the creation of the commission in the
1940s. What the commission said the press should provide has become a familiar litany: a "truthful, comprehensive and intelligent"
account of the daily events, a forum to exchange opinion, an effort to
reflect the attitudes of various groups in the society, a presentation of
the goals and values of society, and an effort to reach all of a society's
members.

The more revolutionary concept in the Hutchins Commission report
is the proposal that the journalism be moral, that its freedom must be
conditioned on its accountability. This does not mean a press that is
constrained, but a press that takes on the burden of moral responsibility on its own initiative. This notion is even more old-fashioned, even
stodgy, and many journalists would cringe at hearing their daily work
described in such terms. Yet the best of journalists want to tell the
truth; they want to do good. Ambition and misguided policy may
sometimes lead them astray, but I have always been impressed at their
belief that they are performing, even humbly, a public service. In
short, they wish to conduct themselves morally.

However, they work in an imperfect, sometimes bewildering and
frequently undemocratic system. The working journalist now customarily sits at the bottom of a management pyramid extending upward
half a dozen or more layers, and it is often hard to pin down individual
responsibility or conscience in a corporate setting.

Inevitably, valid press criticism must line up on the side of individual responsibility. I hope that at the least critics can continue to
come to the aid of the conscience of the individual journalist, when
that person seeks to go beyond what is required by mere law and
economics. I do not see this as partisanship, but rather as sustained,
tight, even stern monitoring of the output of journalists held up to
professional, social and moral criteria.

This should be the primary effort of journalism criticism as we move past the millennium. We will need a criticism that is based in the working journalist's milieu, is morally coherent and is, not least, literate and accessible to all. As long as these are considered vague goals, they can be considered easy of attainment. If they are invoked seriously they may have to run against the tide of the times in an approach that may be difficult, even arduous. That will make them all the more worth pursuing.

James Boylan, professor emeritus of journalism at the Univesity of Massachusetts-Amherst, was founding editor of the Columbia Journalism Review.

The Bumpy Road of Regulation

Achieving editorial freedom in broadcasting and cyberspace

Stuart N. Brotman

WHEN CHAIRMAN W.J. "Billy" Tauzin (R-La.) of the U.S. House Telecommunications, Trade and Consumer Protection Subcommittee banged the gavel to begin oversight hearings on March 17, 1999, those in attendance knew that this was not to be a typical congressional session. The chairman of the Federal Communications Commission, William E. Kennard, was sitting quietly at the witness table, along with his four fellow commissioners from the independent regulatory agency created by Congress in 1934 to regulate broadcasting and telecommunications. They knew that their appearance might be characterized as a trip to the woodshed.

Rep. Tauzin addressed the FCC's worst fears immediately. "The Commission has been operating without statutory authorization since 1991," he noted in his introductory remarks. "It is my hope that this will be the first in a series of public hearings, leading to the introduction of comprehensive FCC reform legislation later this summer."

That was a preamble to the real punch line: "When Congress passed the historic, much-publicized Telecommunications Act of 1996, we made a fundamental mistake. We failed to reform an outdated, out-of-touch Federal Communications Commission when we overhauled the law. As a result, as America prepares to enter the 21st century, we have, in effect, a horse-and-buggy agency trying to bridle supersonic technology. And it's simply not working. Simply put, can an agency created in the 1930s, instilled with a regulatory purpose and ingrained with a regulatory mind-set, effectively oversee the 'deregulatory' policies engineered by Congress for a modern-day marketplace? The answer is no."

Bill Kennard, a Clinton administration appointee who previously had served as the agency's general counsel, listened attentively and waited for his turn to speak. On the table in front of him was a report entitled "A New Federal Communications Commission for the 21st Century," in effect the term paper he and his colleagues had decided to write before having to face the teachers sitting above them at a distance. And in his quiet, lawyerly fashion, the chairman of the FCC began to deliver his response in measured tones: "In . . . a world where old industry boundaries are no longer and competition is king, we need a new FCC. . . . [T]he traditional boundaries delineating the FCC's current operating bureaus will cease to be relevant. Simply, in five years' time, the FCC will be dramatically transformed."

Although much of the focus of this process of reinventing the FCC is on telecommunications rather than electronic media, the broad and deep impact of this "less regulation, less government" paradigm shift also is destined to change the role of the FCC as it oversees program content regulation for broadcast radio and television news and public affairs programming.

In 1999, KENNARD's agency has been the subject of growing scrutiny and withering comments from both House and Senate members, Republicans and Democrats alike. Rumors of legislative drafts float around Capitol Hill, some designed to prevent the FCC from enacting new regulations, others requiring a "super majority" of commissioners before any new rulings could be issued. Moreover, the dollars contemplated to support the FCC's intensified workload since the passage of the new Telecommunications Act are significantly less than what the FCC's budget planners say is necessary to maintain the agency.

As Chairman Kennard noted in his testimony, the FCC in the future will need to focus less on traditional regulatory functions and more on protecting consumers in ways the market itself cannot. Thus, it is abundantly clear that the FCC is destined to become leaner and, correspondingly, have less ability to regulate news and public affairs programming. The only unknown is whether this will happen sooner because of congressional action or later if the FCC is allowed to phase in its proposed five-year restructuring plan.

"Our guiding principle should be to presume that new entrants and competitors should not be subjected to legacy regulation," the FCC's 21st century report asserts. Those involved in broadcast news and public affairs are looking for signs of that principle taking hold. In an age of media convergence, the Internet represents Exhibit A. As text and video images become merged and transmitted to computer terminals as well as conventional television sets, there is no more dramatic or urgent test regarding whether the FCC really understands how the square pegs of technology no longer fit the round holes that segregate broadcasting, cable and satellites. With increasing frequency they are transmitting comparable or identical information services, making the logic of regulating them in different ways difficult to sustain.

Already, in a speech that preceded the oversight hearing by a matter of days, Chairman Kennard stated unequivocally that the FCC for now has decided not to approach regulation of the Internet. In effect, the FCC has decided to invoke the Hippocratic oath with respect to regulating cyberspace—first, do no harm. Speaking publicly before a meeting of telecommunications and Internet analysts, Kennard stated, "I want to say this as clearly as I can . . . as long as I'm chairman of the Federal Communications Commission, this agency will not regulate the Internet." He expressed concern that consumer groups and others already were saying, "the big bad FCC is going to impose all this regulation on the Internet" and noted that he gets "literally about 600 e-mail messages a day by people who are telling me to keep my hands off the Internet."

Cynics argue that despite Kennard's sincerity, the key phrase is "as long as I'm the chairman of the Federal Communications Commission," a tenure that may end with the inauguration of a new president in 2001, if not sooner. Consequently, some members of Congress want to develop a more enduring and secure regulatory firewall by adopting new legislative language that would make explicit that the FCC has no statutory authority to regulate the Internet. Other legislators, however, remain ambivalent about taking the reins off content regulation of the Internet, whether overseen by the FCC or by federal prosecutors. Web access by children remains a potent political issue that attracts headlines and heated debates in the religious, educational and civil liberties communities.

BUT IRONICALLY, IN this area, Congress faces the possibility of being called to the woodshed, too. After all, it is batting 0 for 3 when its

Internet laws have faced federal judges, including the justices of the U.S. Supreme Court, who have ruled that attempts to impose Internet content regulation do not pass constitutional muster. In 1996, a three-judge panel of federal judges in Philadelphia struck down a portion of the Telecommunications Act of 1996 known as the Communications Decency Act (CDA). The CDA had been supported by a bipartisan coalition in Congress and defended by the Clinton administration after the president signed the bill into law. In that decision, Judge Stewart Dalzell struck down provisions that would have restricted "indecent" speech on the Internet as violative of the First Amendment. "As the most participatory form of mass speech yet developed," Judge Dalzell wrote, "the Internet deserves the highest protection from governmental intrusion."

The U.S. Supreme Court agreed, affirming Judge Dalzell's application of the most stringent level of First Amendment review for regulation of Internet content. In a unanimous decision (with Chief Justice Rehnquist and Justice O'Connor concurring in part and dissenting in part), the Court held that "in order to deny minors access to potentially harmful speech, the CDA effectively suppresses a large amount of speech that adults have a constitutional right to receive and to address to one another."

Following this stinging rebuke, Congress and the Clinton administration went back to the drawing board, enacting a new but narrower law that was incorporated into the 1998 budget bill. The Child Online Protection Act (COPA) was challenged immediately by a coalition of 17 organizations and businesses, including the American Civil Liberties Union, which successfully had litigated the CDA, and the Internet Content Coalition, which represents nearly two dozen Web publishers such as *The New York Times*. The law was intended to regulate the availability of sexually explicit material on the Internet that was deemed "harmful to minors" (those under 17 years of age), a standard that, unlike pornography, was given a lesser threshold—namely, "lacking serious literary, artistic, political or scientific value for minors." The law's opponents argued successfully that this definition was too broadly drafted to take effect absent a full trial on the merits, thus warranting an immediate injunction against enforcement.

Even though COPA encompassed only commercial Web sites, and despite its allowing defenses by site providers such as age verification through credit card registration, the journalistic community and other plaintiffs asserted that there was no justification for avoiding the Supreme Court's prior First Amendment bar. After all, Internet news coverage might display controversial works of art, discuss issues related to sexuality and public health or carry items that contained graphic, nonpornographic details.

Federal Judge Lowell A. Reed Jr. reached the same result as had the Supreme Court and Judge Dalzell in the previous case. But he wrote with less sweeping brush strokes than Judge Dalzell, who had painted a picture of the Internet as "a never-ending worldwide conversation." Instead, Judge Reed seemed to encourage Congress not to give up hope. "This Court and many parents and grandparents would like to see the efforts of Congress to protect children from harmful materials on the Internet to ultimately succeed and the will of the majority of citizens in this country to be realized through the enforcement of an act of Congress," he wrote. The Department of Justice has appealed Judge Reed's injunction barring COPA's enforcement to the U.S. Court of Appeals for the 3rd Circuit, which is expected to hear the case later this year.

SO DESPITE STATEMENTS that give rise to a belief that the technological convergence embodied in the Internet inevitably will trump the regulators, it's clear that this debate still has a lot of steam left. As time passes, the Internet's growing pervasiveness as a source of news and information will attract more attention. Journalists, now and in the future, will work for literally thousands of broadcast news services with mirror operations in cyberspace. Will their product be regulated in one medium—broadcasting—but be completely free of restrictions in print or cyberspace? And if reporting displayed on a computer terminal can't be regulated, the body politic will begin to ask questions such as, Why is there a constitutional distinction between Tom Brokaw reporting a story on the "NBC Nightly News" and seeing him through streaming video on the MSNBC Web site?

The U.S. Supreme Court went well beyond the traditional explanation of lesser First Amendment protection for broadcasters due to broadcast spectrum scarcity when it decided in 1978 that the FCC could regulate "indecency" in broadcasting because it was a medium that was "uniquely accessible to children," and "uniquely pervasive in the lives of all Americans." But with personal computers now in the majority of American homes, a national commitment to have them in all schools and libraries, and the development of "always on" Internet connections by leading cable television and telephone companies, it's somewhat difficult to parse why the Supreme Court's affirmance of the FCC's ability to regulate broadcast indecency won't extend to the Internet if the FCC decided to reverse course and the Court chose to apply the same constitutional reasoning. In other words, if the Internet is deemed to be uniquely accessible to children and pervasive to all Americans—a reality that either is here today or soon to come— couldn't such a characterization serve as the constitutional hook that prior Internet regulation schemes have lacked? With this frame of reference, those who express anxiety about how progressive cyberspace jurisprudence really will be are raising serious concerns indeed.

HAVING PEERED INTO the future, let's review the current situation. With respect to today's regulation of broadcast news and public affairs, the glass seems both half full and half empty. For those taking comfort in the FCC's diminishing role as a government editorial gatekeeper, the agency's decision to exempt all news programming from the new V-chip ratings system suggests that the Commission recognizes its need to treat broadcast journalism with extra-sensitive care. So too does the May 1998 ruling by the FCC's Mass Media Bureau that the no-censor-ship provision of the Communications Act of 1934, as amended by the Telecommunications Act of 1996, prohibits the agency from review-ing the news judgments of radio and television stations.

In that case, a citizen's group called Rocky Mountain Media Watch filed petitions to deny the license renewals for the ABC, CBS, NBC and WB network affiliates in the Denver market. The group cited a number of complaints, including a failure to cover community issues adequately, overcommercialization in news programming and stereo-typing of news anchors. Writing on behalf of the FCC, Barbara Kreisman, chief of the Video Services Division, noted that broadcast licensees are "entitled to the widest latitude of journalistic discretion" in presenting news and public affairs information, and presented a number of FCC precedents to support this conclusion. The broadcast-ing community immediately applauded the FCC's decision. "We de-fend the right of stations to exercise editorial judgment in local news coverage," said Eddie Fritts, president of the National Association of Broadcasters (NAB). Barbara Cochran, president of the Radio-Televi-sion News Directors Association (RTNDA) was even more emphatic.

"The FCC's decision supports definitively the editorial freedom of broadcast journalists," she asserted.

What remained hidden from view when these statements were made was the protracted battle both the NAB and RTNDA have been waging against the FCC because they believe that their glass of First Amendment protection really is half empty. After the Fairness Doctrine was eliminated by the FCC in a bold decision in 1987, the regulatory fiat requiring broadcasters affirmatively to air diverse views on "controversial issues of public concern" became a footnote in communications law history. Although there are periodic murmurings among public interest advocates to have the FCC reverse course, the most recent petition requesting this has been languishing at the agency for five years, with no signs of any agency interest in taking action. Congress is not interested in a revival, either, making it safe to assume that the Fairness Doctrine has moved beyond suspended animation to rigor mortis.

BUT IN PRONOUNCING the Fairness Doctrine dead and buried more than a decade ago, the FCC left the doctrine's offspring—the personal attack and political editorializing rules—very much alive. The personal attack rule, developed by the FCC in the 1960s, covers situations where broadcast facilities are used to attack a person or group. According to the FCC, if "the attacks are of a highly personal nature which impugn the character and honesty of named individuals, broadcasters have an affirmative obligation to see to it that the persons attacked are afforded the fullest opportunity to respond." The political editorializing rule gives a right-of-reply to candidates for any elected office when a broadcaster endorses an opponent. Both rules remain on the books and have generated hundreds of enforcement actions against radio and television stations over the years. Despite all the rhetoric of regulatory freedom it delivers to the broadcast community, the FCC has failed to rescind these rules during the last decade and, in doing so, has created confusion in the broadcast journalism community regarding the scope of editorial freedom that is in place.

The NAB and RTNDA asked the FCC to eliminate these rules in 1987, arguing that the Fairness Doctrine's demise due to its chilling effect on broadcasters compelled their rescission as well. By 1996, with no FCC response, these groups filed a federal court appeal asking the judges to mandate that the FCC rule on the matter rather than have it remain in limbo. The U.S. Court of Appeals for the District of Columbia Circuit agreed with this request and ordered the FCC to reach a decision. But the five-member FCC deadlocked on the matter after Chairman Kennard, a former NAB staff attorney, recused himself to avoid a potential conflict of interest.

The NAB and RTNDA now are back in court, arguing that since the FCC hasn't been able to decide even when it was ordered to, the judges should decide the issue on the merits once and for all. The FCC, in its reply brief, argues that preservation of these rules is both reasonable and constitutional.

So DESPITE VISIONS of cyberspace as a long, smooth information highway that rolls on endlessly, the current roadblock of rules regulating broadcast indecency, personal attacks and political editorials suggests that there may be a bumpy road ahead. The FCC, as we have seen, is the least likely regulator to resolve these First Amendment tensions, even if it chose to, because its scope and influence are destined to be diminished. Congress, the agency's overseer, could step in to write its own road map, but even if this happens, the ultimate policy-makers are destined to be the courts. The judicial branch, which is the most removed from the fray, represents the best possible First Amendment guardian for electronic media. But this role only can be assumed if there is a ripe controversy at hand and if there is a judicial willingness to confront the challenge.

Former NBC Executive Vice President and General Counsel Corydon B. Dunham framed the issue with unusual precision. "Whether print, broadcasting, cable, satellite, telephone or the Internet, the real question is: Is it news?" And "[i]f it is," he concludes, "then it should have full First Amendment standing." That's not the law of the land today, but rather an endpoint that I think should be pursued. So hopefully, when this article is retrieved from a time capsule 10 years from now, Rep. Tauzin, Chairman Kennard and all of us will be able to look back at the House Subcommittee's hearings as the starting point of a process. The best oversight will ensure that our deep American instincts supporting free press finally can emerge from the shadows of FCC and congressional intervention.

Stuart N. Brotman teaches entertainment and media law at Harvard Law School and is the author of Communications Law and Practice.

Review Essay

A history of the future of the media

Peering Forward

The conduct of the news media is part of a fretful arc of apprehension that spans the 20th century.

Christopher Dornan

THE PRESENT, OF course, is just the future waiting to happen, but never more so than in the 20th-century West. A culture founded on the promise of perpetual change for the better—in a word, progress—is a culture that can never be satisfied with the way things are, a culture itchy to get on with it, whatever it turns out to be.

No one this side of sanity would dispute that life at the turn of the 20th century is an improvement on life at the turn of the 19th, and yet the 100-year stretch that gave us insulin, television and universal suffrage also gave us Ypres, Auschwitz and the vivid prospect of Mutually Assured Destruction. With that dubious pedigree, the West has been justifiably nervous about what might lie in store even as it hurries to put the past behind it. Small wonder the contours of possible futures have long been a cultural preoccupation.

In come-hither visions of a sleek, bountiful world of wondrous machinery (the 1939 New York World's Fair, *Popular Mechanics* magazine, Disney's Tomorrowland and Epcot) and in art-directed depictions of a world in ruins (the Mad Max movies and every other science fiction scenario set amid radioactive rubble) the 20th century consistently mined the future as a rich vein of popular entertainment. It is no coincidence that over the course of the century, the West elevated popular entertainment to something approaching a *raison d'être*. If anything distinguishes this turn of the century from the last, surely it is the deadly seriousness with which the *fin de millennium*

139

insists on its amusements. ("Do you remember lingerie?" the gyro captain asks Mad Max wistfully in *The Road Warrior*. The joke is that what gives a 20th-century audience the willies is not so much the collapse of order, governance and infrastructure, but the prospect that the party will finally come to an end. There will be no fun anymore, and therefore nothing to live for. The survivors will envy the dead, indeed.)

Among the myriad paradoxes of this gleaming, ghastly century has been the way the emphasis on entertainment has grown even as the more conscientious aspects of journalism and the news media have improved. Despite the litany of complaint about the Fourth Estate at century's end, is there any doubt that the journalism of North America and Western Europe in 1999 is superior to its equivalent circa 1899? As an ongoing archive of the present devoted to putting into play the facts and arguments of civic life, and for all its manifest faults, the journalism of today is simply more scrupulous, more professional, guided by a greater sense of its responsibilities and more aware of its limitations.

If life is better now for those of us lucky enough to inhabit what Michael Ignatieff calls "the zones of safety," this is in no small part because the great, rolling conversation of democracy is more accessible and inclusive—more informed by more people, for more people—and for that we have the media to thank. At the same time, journalism, the record of the real, is both dwarfed by and participant in the unreal carousel of continual media amusement, while the amusements themselves become ever more coarse. Hence the emblematic advent of so-called "reality TV," a chimera of a genre that deploys the deadpan conventions of objective reportage for no higher purpose than shock-horror spectacles of gruesome car crashes and grisly deaths: snuff journalism.

If the sheer prominence of the media in all their multiplying aspects is a badge of the present, we shouldn't be surprised if the media prove to be architectural agents of the onrushing future. But what will a world shaped by media imperatives look like, what place will journalism occupy in such a future, and did anyone see it coming?

The postmodernists would have us believe it is now all but impossible to conceive of what the future will look like, because with the supposed failure of the West's master narratives—among them, a faith in progress—we have no sense of trajectory, and therefore our imaginations are becalmed in the present. But as usual the postmodernists overstate the case for rhetorical effect. The shibboleth of progress is alive and well, and there are powerful agencies with firm designs on the future. What are Microsoft and IBM, if not empires built on the promise of tomorrow? You've got to admit it's getting better, sing the current iMac ads, getting better all the time.

SPECULATIVE FICTION IS not the R&D lab of literature; it does not presume to foretell or shape the contents of an actual tomorrow. Rather, fictions set in a time yet to come inevitably address the concerns of the moment in which they were composed. But revisiting yesterday's fantasies of tomorrow is like sifting through the fossil record of the century's imagination. One can discern patterns of emphasis and anxiety. There is not only a trajectory to history, but a parallel fretful arc of apprehension over the direction in which history might be headed, leading up to the present and pointing into the future. The conduct of the news media have always been central to these worries.

These five works are not the only contenders for the pantheon of speculative fiction, but they would end up on any shortlist. In the multitude of imagined tomorrows, these are the works we are all agreed punctuate the rest. *Looking Backward*, by Edward Bellamy, is a late-19th century utopian reverie, hugely popular in its day, that posits a society utterly rid of the injustices of industrialism. Aldous Huxley's *Brave New World* (1932) and George Orwell's *1984* (1949) are complementary dystopias bracketing the Second World War. Stanley Kubrick and Arthur C. Clarke's *2001: A Space Odyssey* (1968) manages to lovingly celebrate technological progress while simultaneously making it humdrum. William Gibson's *Neuromancer* (published, in one of those neat-o coincidences, in 1984) inaugurated the subgenre of cyberpunk and so, presumably, was onto something.

Looking Backward is already merely a curiosity, its memory pickled in formaldehyde on the reading lists of universities. In its time it was a sensation, translated into more than 20 languages. Only *Ben Hur* and *Uncle Tom's Cabin* were more popular. Today, it falls on tin ears. Quite apart from the fact that the conventions of the contemporary novel have overtaken it, the world whose ills it confronted so as to excite a generation simply no longer exists.

The plot, in a nutshell: Well-to-do young Boston gentleman has insomnia, resorts to mesmerism and specially sealed sleeping chamber. Things go awry. He awakes in the year 2000 in the home of the kindly and wise Dr. Leete, who serves as his guide to the world of the future, mainly by delivering windy speeches over after-dinner cigars. The good doctor has a comely and modern-minded daughter. Apart from a contrived twist late in the day—has this all been but a dream?— the telegraphed romance between our hero and heroine is the novel's sole plot development.

Clearly, to a 19th-century readership painfully aware of the social and environmental costs of industrial capitalism—belching factories, inner-city squalor, a vast, uneducated underclass conscripted to work for paltry wages in dangerous and filthy circumstances—the appeal of *Looking Backward* lay in its sunny depiction of a prosperous and progressive state in which collective well-being has replaced private gain as the motor force of social affairs. In Bellamy's future of plenty, there are no disparities of income or status. Men and women perform work for which they are individually suited and all varieties of labor are equally valued. Without avarice, there is no envy. Without injustice, there is no unrest. The future is a peaceable republic of purpose and fulfilment, replete with technological wonders such as electric lighting and telephonic broadcasting: the New Jerusalem meets Menlo Park.

Bellamy had been a crusading journalist prior to writing *Looking Backward*, and in his idealized future it is not only technology that is liberating but communication technology, and indeed the conduct of the press. Dr. Leete explains that the newspapers of the past were "crude and flippant, as well as deeply tinctured with prejudice and bitterness." Inasmuch as they reflected the public to whom they were addressed, they gave "an unfavorable impression of the popular intelligence, while so far as they may have formed public opinion, the nation was not to be felicitated." Or, to put it in present-day vernacular, they were written as though for morons and caused more harm than good.

In Bellamy's future, newspapers have been liberated from capitalist proprietors who used them to control the course of debate, foisting their self-serving worldviews on a captive public and thereby undermining the democratic project. Readers in the year 2000 not only support the papers of their choice through subscriptions, unhitching journalism from the mule train of advertising, but appoint and dismiss the editors as they see fit. Papers spring up if there is a sufficient constituency for their offerings, while nothing prevents a civic-minded citizen from addressing the greater public by publishing his or her own books and pamphlets. There is an endearing optimism to such a vision of the redemptive powers of the media. It is not simply that a perfect society would be marked by a responsible press devoted to the calm presentation of necessary intelligence and genteel, informed debate, but that just such a responsible press is a precondition of an ideal society. This is an optimism rooted in the conviction that citizens are themselves naturally responsible and rational, and would disdain the base and trivial blandishments of a profit-driven press if given the opportunity.

It is, however, a utopian ideal. (By 1947, the members of the Hutchins Commission on Freedom of the Press admitted that though they might conceive of the perfect newspaper, it would be an artifact the public would never "live up to.") Even Bellamy's notion of a realm of public discourse freed from the dictates of capitalist media barons, with all citizens able and willing to voice their opinions constructively, prefigures the early rhetoric that heralded the advent of the Internet. The Internet was going to undermine the centralized agencies of public address, democratizing communication by conferring the power to publish on anyone with a modem. What was promised was a return to the agora, a reinvigorated public sphere. What we got was triple-X porno sites and Matt Drudge.

What makes *Looking Backward* irredeemably quaint, however, is the complete absence of a cult of celebrity as a defining fact of both the news media and society. Bellamy's hero, Julian West, passes his time in Dr. Leete's household curiously unpestered by reporters. He knows the outside world is aware of his astonishing existence, since he himself listens to a preacher sermonizing about him via telephonic broadcast. But other than that, the media of Bellamy's tomorrow pay no attention to West whatsoever. Had he woken up in the real year 2000, of course, he would have seen camera crews camped out on the lawn as thick as locusts and just as well behaved. Letterman and Leno would be making nudge-nudge jokes about his sex life. The tabs would go nuts: "Century Man may carry deadly virus from the past, scientists warn." CAA would be handling the arrangements for his inevitable interview with Barbara Walters. Perhaps not as bad as waking up in an Orwellian universe with a rat cage strapped to your face, but not a lot of fun either.

HUXLEY'S VERSION OF the future is almost identical to Bellamy's, except Huxley insists no society can be that placidly contented without the aid of jumbo tranquilizers, mindless distraction and limitless sex. Living happily as we do in a world of Ritalin, Prozac, Viagra and the Fox network, it is hard not to concede the point. When it was published, however, *Brave New World* was the *American Psycho* of its day, dismissed as a one-note exercise by a precocious writer making his pornographic point as offensively as possible. That was then. Today, it deserves its reputation as the first and best exploration of what can go wrong even if everything presumably goes right. *Brave New World* is the original un-topia.

And Huxley was nothing if not savvy to how the media might play out in a society exclusively devoted to the pursuit of happiness. In his sexually uninhibited future, folks go to the feelies—just like the movies, but with the added jolt of tactile-emotional input from the screen. Naturally, popular taste in big-budget feelies skews toward melodramas with graphic sex scenes. Cybersex, anyone?

As well, Huxley, unlike Bellamy, calculated on the corrosive effects of celebrity. Extrapolating from his own age—which was already reeling from the rise of the movies, radio, public relations and national brand-name advertising campaigns—Huxley posits a society hypersensitive to small differences of status and intoxicated with fame.

Like *Looking Backward*, *Brave New World* turns on the arrival of an outsider, a man to whom the ways of the future are entirely alien. In this caste-stratified society Bernard Marx is an Alpha Plus psychologist with his eye on the pneumatic Lenina Crowne. He takes her on a date to New Mexico, a Savage Reservation where the indigenous people live as they always have, without the benefit of the social and technological engineering of the outside world. No feelies, no television, no games of Escalator-Squash, no soma, the little grams of bliss the citizens of the future are forever popping at the first twinge of emotional discomfort. Worse, with no hatchery or conditioning laboratories, the savages actually give birth—shudder—and raise their own children. On their trip to the reservation, Bernard and Lenina encounter a woman from their own world, lost and abandoned there years ago when she, like them, was an anthropological tourist. She has a son, John, now a young man, who is scandalously the issue of Bernard's own Director.

John and his mother accompany Bernard and Lenina back to civilization, where the young man—Mr. Savage—becomes an exotic conversation piece, trotted out for the amusement of high society. Bernard uses him to curry favor with his superiors and score with the ladies. Eventually, disgusted with the shallowness of the *Brave New World*, John becomes a hermit. But the world refuses to leave him alone; he is too delicious a curiosity, with his bows and arrows and rituals of self-flagellation.

A reporter from The Hourly Radio, wired for live broadcast, intrudes on his solitude and John sends him packing violently. The assault itself becomes news ("Reporter has coccyx kicked by mystery savage"), which only attracts other correspondents, including the Feely Corporation's ace paparazzo, who spends three days staking him out, hiding microphones in the heather, finally capturing John through telephoto lenses as he whips himself in a frenzy of self-loathing.

The feely is a smash hit, and immediately hordes of gawkers descend on John, urging him to scourge himself. Lenina emerges from the crowd only to have John whip her mercilessly in a puritanically libidinous rage to the delight of the onlookers. The next night the crowds return in even greater numbers, but the savage has hanged himself.

Princess Diana. Jerry Springer. Monica Lewinsky's confession that she felt like throwing herself from a hotel balcony once she realized the jig was up. All the themes of the present are contained in Huxley's imagined future, right down to the baying mob and its surrogates in the media amusing other people to death. The contrast could not be more stark between Huxley's version of the future—which is to say, his acid assessment of his own time—and Bellamy's flawless society. In Bellamy's world, the citizenry finds its gratification in edification. Huxley fingers the dawn of reality TV and portrays a technologically resplendent journalism driven by little more than an intrusive, near sadistic voyeurism.

WHILE JOY IN *Brave New World* is all but a civic duty, in *1984* there is no joy that is not illicit. In both futures, power rests on engineered consent for the prevailing order, but the citizens of Huxley's state genuinely believe themselves to be happy, whereas the citizens of Oceania cannot risk contemplating that they might not be. In the former, there is almost no dissidence because there is no perceived reason to dissent; in the latter potential dissidents disappear in the middle of the night, never to be seen again.

1984 is not so much a critique of the West as a warning about how totalitarian regimes would have no choice but to consciously use the media to enforce a false consciousness. If the media in Bellamy's world are given over to education, and in Huxley's to pure amusement, in Orwell's their purpose is neither. They are the primary instruments of conformity. In such a society, confronted with the discrepancy between what one experiences and what one is told to believe, the prudent citizen denies reality and subscribes to the fiction—and even that is no guarantee of security. This is not to say Orwell was any less prescient than Huxley, but simply that what Orwell describes is Stalinism graced with the techniques of Madison Avenue.

His ear for the catchphrase, honed by years as an essayist and as a producer for the BBC during World War II, is pitch-perfect. Perhaps more than any other writer of our century, Orwell understood the strengths of both propaganda and anti-propaganda. War is Peace. Freedom is Slavery. Ignorance is Strength. Today, these neat, simple mental inversions could be slogans for Benetton ads. ("Image is nothing" proclaims the current Sprite campaign, blithely countermanding the reality that image is so obviously everything.) The Junior Anti-Sex League, the Physical Jerks, the Two Minutes Hate, the Ministry of Love—these could all be names of current rock bands, and possibly are.

In a particularly telling inversion, Orwell's protagonist, Winston Smith, is by occupation a journalist, the equivalent of a copy editor, except that his job entails endlessly unwriting the news so that the archival record conforms to the Party's preferred fictions. There are those who, following Gramsci and Althusser, argue that this is precisely what the work of Western mainstream journalism amounts to—a series of partial and contingent versions of reality structured to validate an inegalitarian social order—except that in the real-world newsrooms of the present, the reporters and editors supposedly are unconscious of the ideological implications of their work.

Winston Smith, by contrast, is well aware of what he is doing; he simply cannot afford the luxury of questioning it. Nonetheless, long before the fashionable squawks of Jean Baudrillard and his acolytes about hyperreality and the simulacrum, Orwell spotted how the realm of representation might be used to dictate the contents of the real, rather than the reverse. That is the point, and the end result, of the newsreels filled with lies. That is the point, and the end result, of Smith's interrogation and torture in Room 101. That is the inherent malevolence of a society in which the contract between the news media and the citizenry—that the former will do their best to render accounts of unfolding reality on which the latter can rely—has been permanently abrogated. It is a world in which the very concept of trust has been exterminated.

IF *LOOKING BACKWARD* is an out-and-out utopian fantasy and *1984* is a grim, dyspeptic screed, what is *2001: A Space Odyssey*? The film is so emotionless for its first two-thirds and then so psychedelic in its final act, it seems to greet the future with a mixture of exuberance and ennui. Like Bellamy's work, *2001* is almost bereft of plot: human primate ancestors awake one morning to find a monolith in their midst, clearly planted there by an alien higher intelligence, and shortly thereafter get the bright idea of using animal femurs as cudgels. Skip ahead to the year 1999. U.S. scientists find an identical monolith buried on the moon, which emits a signal directed at Jupiter. A mission is dispatched to investigate, but the on-board computer kills all but one of the astronauts before being disabled. The remaining crew member reaches his destination and encounters something so cryptic as to occasion late-night dorm-room bull sessions for years after the movie's release.

The liveliest personality in the entire film, of course, is HAL the computer, who turns out to be a psychopath. In that, *2001* recycles a cultural anxiety as old as the Golem myths—our creations, the machines, will take on a life of their own, and it won't be in our best interests—but it also prefigures what has become the core futurist fantasy of the late 20th century. *Brave New World* and *1984* depicted futures respectively seduced and cowed into compliance by the media. *2001* postulated a coming time when reality might be superseded by the imaginative capabilities of intelligent machines.

If the nervous cultural tic of the first three-quarters of the 20th century was that the news media, on which the populace relies to duly document what is real and what is known, cannot in fact be trusted, then the anxiety ratchets up a notch in the late 20th century with the arrival of the *new* media, machines infinitely more sophisticated than the old agencies of mass address. With the rise of the computer and its ancillary technologies of communication, mere reality will pale in comparison to the fabulous realms made possible by software. Why live in the drab old real world with all its disappointments when one can inhabit computer-generated sensoria tailored to one's tastes? And what role for journalism—the record of the real—when reality itself has been abandoned, like a once-fertile valley whose riverbed dried up?

The novel credited with christening this theme—and coining the term cyberspace into the bargain—is William Gibson's *Neuromancer*. A hyperactive noir potboiler full of characters with names like Ratz and the Finn, the novel follows the adventures of Case, a hacker, and his partner Molly, who has technoprosthetics surgically implanted behind mirrored lenses where her eyes should be and retractable talons under her fingernails. The pair have been hired by a hard case named Armitage, who may or may not actually be a former Special Forces officer named Corto, for a bit of skulduggery that involves cracking the security of an Artificial Intelligence entity and...oh, never mind. The point is that when Case jacks into the computer he doesn't get a C:> prompt on a screen. "Dermatrodes" attached to his forehead, he enters a netherworld in which he can see and feel the "ice," or software defences, of the systems he's cracking. He is in cyberspace, "a consensual hallucination" that exists nowhere but in the matrix of interlinked computer memory.

In *Neuromancer*, cyberspace remains a sketchy dimension, but in subsequent explorations of the genre it becomes more and more vivid. In Neal Stephenson's *Snow Crash* (1992), for example, cyberspace assumes the form of the Metaverse, again a consensual hallucination, but this time of a city under construction. Users negotiate the virtual space as avatars, computer-generated facsimiles of themselves. They carouse, they scheme, they have sword fights, while their corporeal selves—their meat—sit slumped in front of computer, goggles strapped to their heads. In Tad Williams' *Otherland* (1996), the experience of cyberspace has become so superior to reality that the care and maintenance of the real world has been allowed to deteriorate. Ethnic groups petition to have their customs and mores encoded in the software of the virtual universe as a means of preserving their traditions, which are dying back in the meat world. In the film *The Matrix* (1999), the twist is that the day-to-day life of the present—getting up, going to work, dining out—is in fact a mental illusion created by Artificial Intelligence machines that have taken over. In reality our bodies are prisoners of the machines, providing them with bioelectric power.

So as the 20th century draws to a close, its signature futurist motif is one of escaping reality into a media-maintained imaginary dimension where all fantasies are possible, all desires can be fulfilled. As the Microsoft ads put it, "Where do you want to go today?" The very question presumes that the answer is elsewhere: somewhere more interesting than here and now.

Journalism, of course, has always sold itself on that promise. Yes, its records and narratives purport to map the real, but a reality to which we would otherwise not have access. Journalism is a society's vicarious eyes and ears, and journalists are its paid witnesses. Via notepad and camcorder, they transport their audiences to cabinet rooms and boardrooms, police precincts and killing zones. The difference is that cyber-capitalism promises passage to places that do not exist.

Though the artificial sensorium of cyberpunk is not yet a reality, and may never be, the genre is arguably closer to what has actually come to pass than its predecessors in speculative fiction. In *Looking Backward, Brave New World* and *1984*, the media are mere adjuncts to a centralized political authority. They service a prevailing order, whether benign or odious. They are crucial but subordinate.

Who could have imagined that the media would come to usurp political authority, buffeting the policy process and decision-makers in the chaotic turbulence of perception? In the United States of America, the most advanced and sophisticated nation on the planet, what matters now is not so much what is done, but how actions play out in the mediascape. Journalism was supposed to provide reliable records of the real. Now, it seems, a stew of journalism, entertainment and infotainment establishes what is taken to be real—not, as the Chomskyites insist, according to some master plan for the manipulation of the masses, but in absurd, directionless and irrational gyrations.

What Huxley and Orwell feared was the dominance of collective order over the individual. What we have arrived at is something close to the end of governance as it was once defined. When the media run the show—when the jabber and the images on the airwaves take precedence over what the images were originally meant to depict—no one is in charge. The order of a previous era has been inverted. It is not as frightening a prospect as Orwell's totalitarianism, but it is unsettling nonetheless.

Where do you want to go tomorrow?

Christopher Dornan is director of the School of Journalism and Communication at Carleton University in Ottawa.

For Further Reading

What's Next?

Abrahamson, David, ed. *The American Magazine: Research Perspectives and Prospects*. Ames: Iowa State University Press, 1995.

Baker, William F., George Dessart and Bill Moyers. *Down the Tube: An Inside Account of the Failure of American Television*. New York: Basic Books, 1999.

Bellamy, Edward. *Looking Backward 2000–1887*. 1888. Reprint, New York: Penguin Classics, 1986.

Beniger, James R. *The Control Revolution: Technological and Economic Origins of the Information Society*. Cambridge: Harvard University Press, 1986.

Carey, James W. *Communication as Culture: Essays on Media and Society*. Boston: Unwin Hyman, 1988.

Cherny, Lynn, and Elizabeth Reba Weise, eds. *Wired Women: Gender and New Realities in Cyberspace*. Seattle: Seal Press, 1996.

Cook, Philip S., Douglas Gomery and Lawrence W. Lichty, eds. *The Future of News: Television, Newspapers, Wire Services, Newsmagazines*. Washington: The Woodrow Wilson Center Press, 1992.

Donahue, Hugh Carter. *The Battle to Control Broadcast News: Who Owns the First Amendment?* Cambridge: MIT Press, 1989.

Flournoy, Don M., and Robert K. Stewart. *CNN: Making News in the Global Market*. Luton, England: University of Luton Press, 1997.

Fuller, Jack. *News Values: Ideas for an Information Age*. Chicago: University of Chicago Press, 1996.

Galtung, Johan, and Richard C. Vincent. *Global Glasnost: Toward a New World Information and Communication Order?* Cresskill, N.J.: Hampton Press, 1992.

Gerbner, George, Hamid Mowlana and Herbert I. Schiller, eds. *Invisible Crises: What Conglomerate Control of Media Means for America and the World*. Boulder, Colo.: Westview Press, 1996.

Gibson, William. *Neuromancer*. New York: Ace Books, 1984.

Herman, Edward S., and Robert W. McChesney. *The Global Media: The New Missionaries of Corporate Capitalism*. Washington: Cassell, 1997.

Hess, Stephen. *International News and Foreign Correspondents*. Washington: Brookings, 1996.

————. *The Washington Reporters*. Washington: Brookings, 1981.

Huber, Peter W. *Law and Disorder in Cyberspace: Abolish the FCC and Let Common Law Rule the Telecosm*. New York: Oxford University Press, 1997.

Huxley, Aldous. *Brave New World*. 1932. Reprint, New York: Perennial Classics, 1998.

Johnstone, John W.C., Edward J. Slawski and William W. Bowman. *The `News People: A Sociological Portrait of American Journalists and Their Work*. Urbana: University of Illinois Press, 1976.

Leonard, Thomas C. *News for All: America's Coming-Of-Age With the Press*. New York: Oxford University Press, 1995.

McCombs, Maxwell, Donald L. Shaw and David Weaver, eds. *Communication and Democracy: Exploring the Intellectual Frontiers in Agenda-Setting Theory*. Mahwah, N.J.: Lawrence Erlbaum, 1997.

Miller, Toby. *Technologies of Truth: Cultural Citizenship and the Popular Media*. Minneapolis: University of Minnesota Press, 1998.

Mosco, Vincent, and Janet Wasko, eds. *The Political Economy of Information*. Madison: University of Wisconsin Press, 1988.

Orwell, George. *1984*. 1949. Reprint, New York: Signet Classics, 1950.

Picard, Robert G., and Jeffrey H. Brody. *The Newspaper Publishing Industry: A Turning Point*. Boston: Allyn and Bacon, 1997.

Rosten, Leo C. *The Washington Correspondents*. New York: Arno Press, 1974.

Schwarz, Ted. *Free Speech and False Profits: Ethics in the Media*. Cleveland: Pilgrim Press, 1996.

Smith, Anthony. *The Age of Behemoths: The Globalization of Mass Media Firms*. New York: Priority Press Publications, 1991.

Sunstein, Cass R. *Free Markets and Social Justice*. New York: Oxford University Press, 1997.

————. *Democracy and the Problem of Free Speech*. New York: Free Press, 1993.

————. *After the Rights Revolution: Reconceiving the Regulatory State*. Cambridge: Harvard University Press, 1990.

Turow, Joseph. *Breaking Up America: Advertisers and the New Media World*. Chicago: University of Chicago Press, 1997.

Underwood, Doug. *When MBAs Rule the Newsroom: How the Marketers and Managers Are Reshaping Today's Media*. New York: Columbia University Press, 1993.

Voakes, Paul S. *The Newspaper Journalists of the '90s*. Reston, Va.: American Society of Newspaper Editors, 1997.

Weaver, David H. *The Global Journalist: News People Around the World*. Cresskill, N.J.: Hampton Press, 1998.

Weaver, David H., and G. Cleveland Wilhoit. *The American Journalist in the 1990s*. Mahwah, N.J.: Lawrence Erlbaum, 1996.
———. *The American Journalist*. 2nd ed. Bloomington: Indiana University Press, 1991.

Subject Index

A

ABC News, 16, 115
  buy out of, 118
  decline of, 64
  digital television uses, 68
  license renewal objections, 134
  outsourcing news, 65
Accuracy in Media (AIM), 124
America Online, CBS and, 69
American Civil Liberties Union (ACLU),
  132
American Journalism Review, 124
American Society of Newspaper Editors
  (ASNE), 34, 126
Anonymous sources, refusing use of, 11,
  14
Ash, Timothy Garton, 22
Atlantic Monthly magazine, 54
Audit Bureau of Circulation, 56

B

Bagdikian, Ben H., 125
Balkan states war, 106-107
Baranczak, Stanislaw, 26
Barnicle, Mike, 42
Barrett, Edward W., 122
BBC, 64, 105
Becker, Leo, 32
Bellamy, Edward
  future view of, 142-143
  social capitalism and, 142
  writing plot of, 141-144
  writings of, 141
Benchley, Robert, 122

Bigart, Homer, 123
Bleyer, Willard, 30
Bloomberg news service, 83, 91
Boating magazine, 55
Bode, Ken, 116-119
Bork, Robert, 23
Bosnia, war coverage of, 99
Boston Globe, 42
  Bosnia coverage, 99
  journalism teaching moment, 117
Bowman, William, 31
Brill, Steven, 124
Brill's Content, 124-125
Broder, David, 117
Brokaw, Tom, 133
Business news
  capital for, 92
  challenge for, 95
  China importance, 93
  global business growth, 95
  increasing of, 92
  international news reconfiguring for,
  94
  reader expectations, 93
  reporter questions broadening, 94-95

C

Cable networks
  digital television, 68
  vs network news, 66
CAP Cities, 118
Car and Driver magazine, 55
Cardoso, President, 92
CBS News, 41

155

America Online and, 69
decline of, 64
impeachment vs football, 63
license renewal objections, 134
outsourcing news, 65
vs internet digitized, 68-69
Chicago Tribune, Bosnia coverage, 99
Child Online Protection Act (COPA), 132
Children, Internet access issues, 131-132
China, business reporting importance, 93
Cincinnati Enquirer, journalism teaching
moment, 117
and Chiquita Banana, 117
Civic journalism, 13
Clinton impeachment
journalism after, 20
presidency erosion, 20-21
public reactions to, 11
vs football broadcast, 63
Clinton, President Bill
new president attacking, 22
Starr report survival, 16
Clooney, George, 65
CNBC
individualized interest and, 64
revamping of, 68-69
CNN
critiquing media, 124
journalism teaching moment, 117
news-on-demand, 67-68
network outsourcing to, 64
other media news for, 65-66
ratings impact on, 24
Tailwind debacle, 42
Web site of, 16
Cochran, Barbara, 134
Columbia Journalism Review, 122-124
Commission on Freedom of the Press
government vs media, 127
journalism morals, 127
news responsibility, 127
Committee of Concerned Journalists, 126
Communications Decency Act, 132
Cooke, Janet, 42, 123
Cowan, Geoffrey, 119
Critiquing media
agenda lacking in, 126
benefits of, 121
criteria for, 125
elements lacking in, 125-126

employer criticism, 123
examples of, 122
Hutchins Commission, 127
individual responsibility, 127
internal ombudsmen, 123
journalist action focus, 126
primary effort in, 127-128
publications for, 124-125
reactions from, 123-124
reform goals from, 125
reorienting from, 126-127
social questions focus, 126
television critiques, 124
Cronkite, Walter, 66

D
Dahrendorf, Ralf, 25
Daily Telegraph, Bosnia coverage, 99
Dallas Morning News
Bosnia coverage, 99
rumors in, 84
Dalzell, Judge Stewart, 132
Day, Benjamin, 30
De Soto, Hernando, 22
Democracy
Clinton scandal and, 22
democratic life eroding, 23-25
institution degrading, 21
integrity undermining of, 23
journalism and, 26
journalism relating with, 11
journalists' defense of, 19
presidency erosion, 20-22
virus infecting, 20-21
vs economic efficiency, 25-26
vs new media, 23
vs other significant events, 22-23
Detroit News, 93
Deutsche Welle, 105
Digital television
broadcast news and, 68
cable networks and, 68
entertainment impact of, 68
news rebroadcasting, 68
Disney Corp., 118
Dow Jones news service, 83, 91
Drudge, Matt, 42, 45, 47, 85
Duffy, Michael, 117
Dunham, Corydon B., 136

E

Ebony magazine, 54
Economic world
   authoritarian vs totalitarian, 25-26
   democratic institutions and, 26
   vs liberty, 25
   vs politics, 25
Economist magazine, 92
Editors
   assumption of, 46
   Internet publishing and, 46
   marketplace power and, 46
Edwards, Douglas, 65
Eisenhower, President Dwight, 65
Ellsberg, Daniel, 48
Esquire magazine, 54
Evening Transcript, 30

F

Fairness
   institutional media and, 49
   Internet publishing and, 49
Fairness and Accuracy in Reporting
   (FAIR), 124
Fairness Doctrine, FCC ruling on, 135-
   136
Federal Communications Commission
   (FCC)
   cyberspace regulating, 131
   Fairness Doctrine ruling, 135-136
   guiding principles for, 130-131
   local news discretion, 134
   quiz-show scandal, 66
   reforms of, 129-130
   regulatory vs consumer protections,
   130
   V-chip rating exemptions, 134
   vs citizen groups, 135
Filers. *See* Reporters
Financial Times, 91-92, 94
First Amendment
   broadcaster protections, 133-134
   Internet and, 132, 136
   Internet publishing and, 50
   justification for, 26
   newspaper owners actions, 11-12
   public trust vs economic right, 24-25
   writings on, 125
Flying magazine, 55
Fortune magazine, 31
Fox News, regional news testing, 67

Franklin, Benjamin, 29
"Free Press, Fair Project," 126-127
Freedom Forum, 126
Friendly, Fred W., 125
Fritts, Eddie, 134

G

Gibson, William
   future vision of, 148-149
   writings of, 141
Gingrich, Newt, 66
Glass, Stephen, 42
Goldstein, Tom, 120
Government, journalism relationship with,
   11

H

Halberstam, David, 123
Harper's Magazine, 54
Hearst publishers, 55
Hearst, William Randolph, 41, 45
Hess, Stephen, 31
Hill, Anita, 23
24-hour news
   content of, 84-85, 86
   Drudge and, 85
   financial uses of, 84
   Internet and, 83
   journalistic standards, 86
   "Lewinsky" danger from, 84
   market downturns and, 84-87
   news revolution from, 83-84
   skepticism about, 87
   speed culture for, 85, 87-88
   Wall Street uses of, 83
   wire services as, 83
Houston Chronicle, Bosnia coverage, 99
Hutchins Commission
   journalist education requirements, 31
   See also Commission on Freedom of
   the Press
Huxley, Aldous
   celebrity's corrosive effects, 144
   future view of, 144
   writings of, 141
   writings plot of, 144-145
Hynes, Terry, 120

I

Important stories
   Internet publishing of, 48

resources for, 48
vs large news organizations, 48-49
International reporting
  business news increasing, 92
  business news transforming, 92-93
  business reader expectations, 93
  business vs news reconfiguring, 94
  challenges for, 95
  China importance, 93
  declining of, 91-92
  global business news growth, 95
  reporter question broadening, 94-95
  Soviet Union collapse, 91
Internet
  central reality of, 15
  children's access to, 131-132
  digitizing of, 68-69, 105-106
  FCC regulation of, 131
  financial news availability, 83
  First Amendment and, 132
  global medium of, 104
  importance of, 15
  information gatekeepers of, 16
  journalism skills for, 84
  journalistic standards battles, 86
  laws for, 131-132
  mass media cost, 45
  news information from, 10
  news media on, 68-69
  news revolution from, 83-84
  news sites on, 16
  radio signals receiving, 103-104
  radio's future with, 105-106
  reporter roles, 3-4
  standards and, 12
  vs newspapers, 79
  vs wire services, 83
Internet Content Coalition, 132
Internet magazines
  commercialization of, 58-59
  commitment predictability, 59-60
  specialization trends in, 57-58
  women on-line and, 60
Internet publishing
  editors missing in, 46
  fairness in, 49
  First Amendment and, 50
  traditional media with, 50
  truth vs fiction, 46-47
  vs important stories, 47-49
  vs journalists, 45-46

Investigative reporting
  local focus in, 6
  market size and, 6
  media ownership and, 5-6
  sources for, 6
Irwin, Will, 122
iVillage Web site, 68

J
Johnson, John H., 54
Johnson, Samuel, 47
Johnstone, John, 31
Journalism
  changes in, 9-10
  citizen activity renewals, 12-13
  civic journalism, 13
  civic responsibility reclaiming, 12
  clean news, 5
  Clinton scandal and, 20-21
  cost of, 10, 45
  credibility in, 13-14
  crisis in, 24
  democracy and, 19
  destruction of, 20
  First Amendment meaning, 24-25
  fragmentation in, 9-10
  government relationships with, 11, 20
  information gatekeepers as, 16
  information improvements, 14
  Internet growth and, 15
  investigative news, 5-6
  justification for, 26
  national consensus lacking, 6-7
  news editing, 5
  newspaper differentiation, 13
  other media supporting, 10
  personalization of, 7
  political institution degradation, 21
  politics role in, 23-24
  reader attitudes changing, 12
  scandals propagating by, 11
  skepticism lacking, 24
  standards enforcing, 12
  story focus, 14
  story impact, 6
  student expectations of, 7
  survival of, 16-17
  totalitarianism destroying, 19-20
  vs corporatization, 10-11
  vs entertainment state, 20
  young readership fractionalizing, 15-16

"Journalism Credibility Project," 126
Journalism education
    24-hour news preparing, 115-116
    ethics in, 120
    information specialization, 112
    Internet searching, 113
    interview teaching, 113
    journalism challenge, 115
    journalism environment, 118
    media environment understanding, 113
    media outlets inroads, 114-115
    mid-career education, 119
    "power watchdog" as, 114
    prospects of, 116-117
    public purpose of, 120
    purpose of, 115, 117-119
    technology costs, 113
    technology influencing, 112
    vs fame, 120
Journalism future
    Bellamy's vision of, 141-143
    cultural preoccupation, 139
    Gibson's vision of, 148-149
    governance ending, 149-150
    Huxley's vision of, 144-145
    journalism's promise, 149
    Kubrick's vision of, 147-148
    media-maintaining imaginary, 149
    Orwell's vision of, 145-147
    paradoxes of, 140
    political authority usurping, 149
    postmodernists' approaches, 140-141
    speculative fiction and, 141-142
    visions of, 139-140
Journalist. *See* Minority journalists; Reporters
Journalist, 30

K
Kalb, Bernard, 124
Kalb, Marvin, 111
Kansas, Dave, 81
Keller, Larry, 4
Kelley, Jennifer, 111
Kennard, William E., 129
    appointment of, 130
    Congressional testimony of, 130-131
    FCC scrutiny, 130
    Internet regulations, 131
    See also Federal Communications Commission

Kennedy, President John, 20
Kliesch, Ralph, 33
Kosicki, Jerry, 32
Kosovo, predictability of, 101-102
Kreisman, Barbara, 134
Kubrick, Stanley
    future vision of, 147-148
    works of, 141
Kundera, Milan, 26
Kurtz, Howard, 124, 126

L
Ladies' Home Journal, 53
League of Publishers movement, 13
Lewinsky, Monica
    24-hour news and, 84
    leaking about, 85
    on-line readers and, 16
Liebling, A. J., 47, 122-123
Life magazine, 53-55
Lindstrom, Carl E., 122
Lippmann, Walter, 122
Look magazine, 53-55
Los Angeles Times, 115, 117, 126
Lukas, J. Anthony, 123
Lycos, 58

M
McManus, Doyle, 117
Magazine Publishers of America, 56
Magazines
    business strategy, 53-54
    commitment predictability, 59-60
    decline factors, 55
    form adaptability, 61
    future determining factors, 56
    "golden age" of, 53
    impact of, 53
    Internet trends, 57-61
    proliferation of, 55-56
    profitability of, 56-57
    social reality from, 54-55
    specialized readerships, 55
    unique types of, 54
    women and, 60-61
Matthews, Chris, 84
Mencken, H. L., 39
Men's Health, 56
Meredith Corp., 118
Minority journalists
    changes from, 11

political learning of, 36
quantity of, 33-34
radio use of, 34
religious backgrounds, 36
See also Reporters
Moonves, Leslie, 66
Mott, Frank Luther, 30
Ms. magazine, 56
MTV, digital television uses, 68
Murdoch, Rupert, 25, 41, 45
Murray, Alan, 117

N
Nation, 31
National Association of Broadcasters (NAB)
Fairness Doctrine, 135-136
local news support, 134-135
vs FCC, 135
National News Council, 123
NBC News
decline of, 64
license renewal objections, 134
vs Internet digitized, 68-69
Network news
cable television competition, 64-65
Cronkite era, 66
digital television shifting, 68-69
end of, 64
future of, 67
history of, 65
Internet merging of, 68
network losses, 64
news-on-demand, 67-68
niche focus of, 64
outsourcing of, 65
quiz-show scandal and, 66
regional news and, 67
talent pool for, 65
viewership declining, 63-64
vs all-news cable, 66
vs cable news, 66
vs Clinton scandal, 63
Nevins, Allan, 122
New media, vs democratic institutions, 23
New Republic, 42
New York magazine, 53, 56
New York Times, 3, 41, 47
important stories and, 48
Internet access and, 132
national editions of, 73

news costs of, 5
standards of, 112
war coverage, 98
New York Tribune, 30
New York World, 30
New Yorker magazine, 54, 115
critiquing media in, 122
News. *See* Important stories
Newspaper profitability
administrative changes, 74
advertising customer changes, 74
advertising inserts, 74
outsourcing, 74
Web sites for, 75
Newspaper trends
conservative operations, 77
constituency offending, 77
customer wants, 76-77
success factors, 79-80
Newspapers
advertising declining, 73
central cities vs suburbs, 72
change factors for, 71-73
concentration increasing, 78
differentiation between, 13
features vs news, 75-76
functions of, 71
future of, 77
internal changes, 73
managers focus, 76-77
profitability of, 73-75
readership declining, 72
revenue changes, 77
success factors for, 79-80
Sunday edition stability, 75
vs competition, 71
vs Internet growth, 79
vs television, 78
Web sites for, 75
weekday special interest, 75
world news coverage, 76
Newsweek magazine
Lewinsky story holding, 85
war coverage, 99
Nixon, President Richard, 20, 65

O
O'Connor, Justice, 132
Ohio Press Association, 31
Orwell, George
future view of, 145-147

writings of, 141
Outside magazine, 51, 64

P

Parade magazine, 75
PBS, digital television uses, 68
PC Magazine, 56
PC World, 56
Pentagon Papers, publishing of, 48
Pew Charitable Trusts, 126
Pew Research Center, 11
Pilot magazine, 55
Playboy magazine, 54
Pollak, Richard, 123
Pope, Kyle, 51
Project for Excellence in Journalism, 126
Psychology Today, 56
Pulitzer, Joseph, 30

R

Radio
    digitizing of, 105-106
    international broadcasts, 105
    Internet blending with, 104, 106-107
    Internet transforming of, 103-104
    limitations of, 104
    midterm future for, 105
    minorities in, 34
    popularity of, 104
Radio Australia, 105
Radio B92
    Balkan state war, 106
    jamming of, 106
    vs Yugoslavian government, 107
    Web broadcasts by, 107
Radio-Television News Directors Association (RTNDA)
    Fairness Doctrine and, 135-136
    local news support, 134-135
    vs FCC, 135
Rather, Dan, 63
RCS (Radio Corporation of Singapore), 105
Readers Digest magazine, 54
Reagan, President Ronald, 22
Reed, Judge Lowell A., 133
Regulations
    broadcasters protections, 133-134
    broadcasting vs Internet, 133
    children vs Internet access, 131-133
    Fairness Doctrine and, 135-136

FCC reforms, 129-131
First Amendment and, 136
public affairs discretion, 134-135
Rehnquist, Justice, 132
Reporters
    aging of, 34-35
    apprenticeship system, 29
    characteristics of, 41
    concerns of, 41-42
    credentials for, 40-41
    criteria for, 39-40
    defined, 42-43
    elite, 34
    elitist views of, 40
    free-lance contracts, 4
    future description of, 37
    future source for, 29
    graduate degrees of, 31-32
    independent outsiders and, 41
    jobs for, 3
    minorities and, 33-34
    occupational respect, 30
    political leanings of, 35-36
    professionalism goals, 42
    public confidence and, 42
    purpose of, 40
    religious backgrounds, 36
    search engines and, 3-4
    social responsibility of, 30-31
    studies on, 31
    "typical" descriptions of, 37
    values of, 43
    vs information multiplicity, 40
    women, 30, 32-33
    See also Minority journalists; Stringer reporters
Reuters news service, 83, 91-92
Rivers, William, 31
Road & Track magazine, 55
Rocky Mountain Media Watch, 134
Rosten, Leo, 31, 35
RTM (Malaysian state broadcaster), 105
Rubin, David, 112-114
Ruggles, Robert, 120
Russell, Charles Edward, 122

S

Sail magazine, 55
Salon magazine, 59
Saturday Evening Post, 53, 55

Saturday Review, 122
Scandal
    24-hour news and, 84
    anonymous sources and, 11, 14
    See also Clinton Impeachment
Schell, Orville, 109, 114-116
Schudson, Michael, 30
Scott, Sir Walter, 26
Seldes, George, 122
Self magazine, 56
Shaw, David, 126
Shaw, George Bernard, 40
Simpson, O. J., 23
Ski magazine, 55
Skiing magazine, 55
Slawski, Edward, 31
Smith, Patricia, 42
SNAP Web site, 68
Soviet Union, collapse of, 97
Sports Illustrated magazine, 54
Starr, Kenneth
    leaks from, 85
    new president attacking, 22
Starr report, on-line readers reactions, 16
Stone, I. F., 47, 123
Street.com Web site, 64
Stringer reporters
    benefits of, 99
    broker for, 4
    free-lance contracts, 4
    media using, 99
    problems for, 100
    war news reporting, 98-100
Sun, 30
Swayze, John Cameron, 65

T
Tailwind, 42
Tauzin, W. J. "Billy," 129
Television
    vs newspapers, 78
    See also Digital television
Thomas, Clarence, 23
Time magazine, 41, 54, 66, 117
    war coverage of, 99
Times (London), Bosnia coverage, 99
Times Mirror publishers, 55
Time Warner, Web site cost, 60
de Tocqueville, Alexis, 29

Tripp, Linda, leaks about, 84
Truth
    Internet publishing and, 46-47
    public understanding of, 47
TV Guide magazine, 54

U
U. S. Supreme Court, Internet restrictions
    and, 132
United Press International, 76
U.S. News & World Report, Bosnia cov-
    erage, 99
USA Today, 16, 73
USA Weekend, 75

V
V-chip, FCC and, 134
Voice of America, 105

W
Wall Street, 24-hour news for, 83
Wall Street Journal
    foreign news coverage, 76
    journalists work at, 47
    national editions of, 73
    rumors in, 84
    standards of, 117
Walters, Barbara, Lewinsky interview, 20,
    24
War news reporting
    detailed reporting in, 98
    foreign correspondent quantities, 98
    global shrinking, 97
    Kosovo and, 101-102
    old vs new conflicts, 97
    stringer reporters for, 98-100
    thinking differently about, 100-101
Washington Journalism Review, 123
Washington Post
    critiquing media in, 124
    journalistic work at, 47-48
    ombudsman for, 123
    standards of, 112, 117
WB Network, license renewal objections,
    134
Wells, John, 65
Wilhoit, G. Cleveland, 31, 37
Wire service, vs Internet, 83
Wired magazine, 51, 64
Wisner, George, 30

Women
  as reporters, 30
  elite journalist and, 32-33
  Internet magazines and, 60-61
  journalism changes from, 11
  journalism defections by, 33
  journalism school enrollments, 32
  minority quantities of, 33
  political leanings of, 35-36

Women's International Press Association, 30
World Wide Web. *See* Internet

Y
Yahoo, 3, 58

Z
Ziff-Davis publishers, 55